Praise for *Claim Your Crown*

"Whether you believe you deserve a crown or not, whether you're single, married, young, or old, you are royalty. You deserve to know that you have a seat at a table set for the King, and this book will take you on that journey so you can claim your crown."

Jamie Grace, actress, podcaster, and award-winning singer-songwriter, from the foreword

"*Claim Your Crown* speaks to the truth of who we really are. I believe the key to unlocking joy, purpose, and peace is discovering what it means to be daughters of the King. This book will be a guide to walk you through that journey!"

Kristen Dalton Wolfe, bestselling author of *The Sparkle Effect*, founder of *She Is More*, and former Miss USA

"Tarah-Lynn does a beautiful job of speaking directly to women like they are her sistas. She holds nothing back from telling radical truths in a way that invites us to claim our royal positions as daughters to the King. While reading these words, I was inspired and empowered to have more conversations with Jesus and encouraged to share the love that I've received with others!"

Chelsea Hurst, cohost of the *Encounter Now* podcast and author of *Above All Else*

Love
Letters
FROM THE
King

Love Letters
FROM THE
King

100 DEVOTIONS FOR
THE GIRL WHO WANTS
TO HEAR FROM GOD

TARAH–LYNN
SAINT–ELIEN

Revell

a division of Baker Publishing Group
Grand Rapids, Michigan

Published by Revell
a division of Baker Publishing Group
PO Box 6287, Grand Rapids, MI 49516-6287
www.revellbooks.com

Printed in China

Library of Congress Cataloging-in-Publication Data
Names: Saint-Elien, Tarah-Lynn, author.
Title: Love letters from the King : 100 devotions for the girl who wants to hear from God / Tarah-Lynn Saint-Elien.
Description: Grand Rapids, Michigan : Revell, a division of Baker Publishing Group, [2021]
Identifiers: LCCN 2020045299 | ISBN 9780800736965 (cloth)
Subjects: LCSH: Young women—Prayers and devotions. | Young women—Religious life. | Christian women—Prayers and devotions. | Christian women—Religious life.
Classification: LCC BV4551.3 .S35 2021 | DDC 242/.633—dc23
LC record available at https://lccn.loc.gov/2020045299

21 22 23 24 25 26 27   7 6 5 4 3 2 1

To Skai, Nylah, Rebekah, Zariah, Tabby, and Emma-Lee:
My queens-to-be, may you grow strong
in the love of our Lord.

And to every girl who has ever loved before,
I pray God wraps you in His arms with the real thing!

Introduction

There was a time when house phones—yes, house phones—would ring, and a girl would sprint to pick up the call before anyone else could. It all started out with full-fledged enthusiasm . . . until she discovered it wasn't him.

Looking down, God often found His daughter wringing her hands and staring at the phone as the minutes ticked right on by. Sometimes the guy would call. Sometimes there'd be an excuse. Sometimes there'd be no communication at all.

During the wait, she wondered, *What is he doing? Is he into me? Did he find someone else? Am I not his type?*

God always called to assure His daughter of His attention, but He never got an answer.

When cell phones came around, she wondered if the guy would text first, if at all. She was willing to spend all her prepaid minutes on him. They'd spend hours on the phone until they were disconnected by force. And even when prepaid minutes weren't an issue, she wondered, *Am I the only one he's talking to?*

God called; God texted. Yet He received no response from her.

Then things changed again.

Today we call it the "slide into my DMs" approach. You know, when a user sends a direct message to you with the motive of expressing their interest. If you are interested, you respond favorably and take it from there.

But sometimes there's no direct message from him at all. Sometimes it's a mixed signal. Nevertheless, she's left with shattered hopes, idle fingers, and tear-soaked pillows.

I get it.

Whether the guy who broke your heart was your crush, your significant other, or your birth father, God's love will cut through any feeling of not being "good enough" to be seen, loved, secured, and treasured. There are many messages out there—many deterring you from the truth. But God is always calling and writing and texting a message of love just to let you know it's always been Him.

I wrote *Love Letters from the King* for girls searching for answers to their daily struggles as shared on social media. Our loving Father and King speaks directly to our situations, while forming a refuge around us and repelling conflicting messages.

And so, each devotion was created to push you to growing in God and living a life you love full of abundance and victory. As you wrestle with issues of identity, intimacy, pain, and perseverance, I've provided an appendix in which you can easily select the girl you resonate most with every day. You won't have to google what you need; you'll find God's tender lovingkindness right here.

Likes, comments, and direct messaging are how we mainly communicate today, and I've embraced it in this book. *Love*

Letters from the King illustrates that while God's answers may not always be instant, He always speaks directly to our hearts. It showcases that God can speak on- and off-screen. It also proves that a DM from our King is much more special than receiving a DM from anyone else! No one can love us and show us attention the way God can, and He always welcomes us to open conversation. I pray you feel God personally singling you out to write a love letter that'll speak to your situation and soothe your soul.

Girl, you have a King who will reach out to you directly. He sends clear messages, so you won't ever have to worry about playing the guessing game. He won't keep you waiting by your phone, wondering if you're on His mind. You'll get a text back—in fact, He will even reach out first.

He desires that we filter out the lies, confusion, heartbreak, and expectations of the world and feast on His living Word. It is my hope that in reading this devotional day to day, you will learn to never settle about any aspect of your life. Page by page, you'll discover the realities of your royal station. You'll discover the overwhelming love of Jesus, your King, and you will begin to look for His messages wherever you go.

Though the modes of communication have changed, God will utilize any platform to get His message across to you. In fact, He has already sent them. All that's left for you to do is open up and receive.

Will you leave His messages on "read" or will you respond?

God speaks, but sometimes we're so busy with everything else that we neglect to answer. We forget the sound of His voice altogether or, in some cases, never knew it in the first place. But as in every relationship, our communication with Christ has to be two-sided to work. Won't you take this time to focus on redirecting your heart to the One who's been waiting on you all along? Are you ready to reduce the clutter of your inbox and soak in the reality of His love? The King of the universe wants to immerse you in His.

He wants you to know there's no love on earth like the love He freely gives. He is the Father who chases after you. He is the Father who is ever so mindful of you. He is the Father who will always come home.

In fact, daughter of the King, you'll always find your home in Him.

God is bringing
a freshness
to your life
that you can't
even imagine!
Are you
ready for it?

one

You Were Made for More

"Blah." That's exactly how I feel. There's this gaping emptiness in my chest—one that pushes me to look for something, someone to fill it. Wintertime often reminds me of that void. It's a thing, you know? "Winter blues," they call it. Scientists say we are more prone to feeling this way in the colder seasons because our bodies miss the sun. But even when the snow melts and I begin to feel glorious rays on my skin, I wonder, *How is it that a hole can feel so heavy?* —*the girl who feels empty*

Hey girl,

You are desperate for more because you were made for more. That void can't be filled with things or people. That ache inside of you is for God; it's for something that lasts in this life and the next.

This God-sized hole nudges at all of humanity, saying, "You aren't home yet." You ache for a love that only He can give. This emptiness points you to your heavenly Father. It is so pervasive that it encourages you to fight to find your way back to Him. Not to that guy or to that thing. No, return to Him.

God will be your home away from home. He will fill you up until you overflow. He will part the clouds and show you His Son in every season. God is who you are missing. And girl—He misses you too.

SCRIPTURE: "He has made everything beautiful in its time. He has also set eternity in the human heart; yet no one can fathom what God has done from beginning to end." (Eccles. 3:11 NIV)

DIG DEEPER: John 3:16; Ephesians 2:10; Colossians 1:16

PRAYER: Heavenly Father, I am running back to You with my aching heart. This world is not my home, and I recognize the hunger and thirst I have for You. I look to You—not to anything in this world—to fulfill me. I crave to know You more and more, and I look forward to greater revelation as I journey through this life and into the next. Thank you for shining Your love down on me in all seasons of my life. Heaven awaits me, and that's something I can get excited about forever. In Jesus's name, amen.

KINGDOM KEY: Pleasure won't satisfy you; living for God's purpose will.

two

God's Love Is Free

I try to be a "good" person. I go the extra mile for people. My community service hours are commendable, and I'm always in search of other ways I can give back. Whenever I slip up and fall into sin, I try my best to make up for it. But sometimes, I feel like my best is not enough, that nothing I do will ever be enough. I'm working on that too. —*the girl who's making up for things*

Hey girl,

You've probably noticed that many religions focus on deeds— your good deeds must outweigh your bad deeds. God's love is not like that.

You don't have to pay Him back. You don't have to "make up" to Him after you've made a mistake. He requires you to repent, not repair. The fixing—the forgiveness—is His job. Whenever you fall, go to your Father.

God admires your grit and applauds how you honor your gifts in service to Him. But do the work because you love Him, not because you want Him to love you. He has already given you His heart. You're not saved by your own works but by what Christ did on the cross.

Christ conquered sin and death, and He's transforming your entire inner being; He works in you and through you.

Stop working for His love; start working in the name of it. Show the world what He has done and can do through you and me.

SCRIPTURE: "God saved you by his grace when you believed. And you can't take credit for this; it is a gift from God. Salvation is not a reward for the good things we have done, so none of us can boast about it. For we are God's masterpiece. He has created us anew in Christ Jesus, so we can do the good things he planned for us long ago." (Eph. 2:8–10)

DIG DEEPER: John 6:28–29; Romans 5:8; James 2:26; 1 John 2:2

PRAYER: Heavenly Father, all of my life I've felt like I've had to overcompensate. I want to be seen a certain way, so I'm scared of making mistakes. I hate feeling like I've let people down. I now realize I've taken that attitude into my relationship with You. Forgive me. I'm grateful for Your sacrificial love, and I look forward to my new journey of working because of Your love, not for it. In Jesus's name, amen.

KINGDOM KEY: Stop working for God's love; start working because of it.

three

He Can Carry That

I'm overworked. I'm overwhelmed. I'm over it. My never-ending to-do list is in competition with matters of my heart. From my family, work, and school to my own personal issues—I'm pulled in every direction, and there's always something that's left to do. There's no way I can keep on going like this. I'm backpacking up a slippery slope, and I'm tired of trudging without gaining any ground. No one on earth can handle the weight of how I feel.
—*the girl with a lot of baggage*

Hey girl,

I may not be able to feel your pain, but I can direct you to the One who experienced it all: Jesus. In carrying that splintered cross, Christ carried the sins of humanity on the long road of sorrow to Golgotha. He knows all too well what it feels like to trudge on with crippling pressure.

He paid the debt for our sins and still wants to take on every single thing we struggle with today. So tell me: If God can carry the weight of the world on His shoulders, can't He carry yours?

The Lord will lighten your load; He can handle the heftiness. Turn your written to-do lists into spoken cries to your Father. Allow Him to carry your hurts, your burdens, your heart. He wants it all today, tomorrow, the next day, and the next year. He wants it whenever you feel you can handle it and whenever you feel you can't. He still wants it all so that He can get to you.

SCRIPTURE: "Then Jesus said, 'Come to me, all of you who are weary and carry heavy burdens, and I will give you rest. Take my yoke upon you. Let me teach you, because I am humble and gentle at heart, and you will find rest for your souls. For my yoke is easy to bear, and the burden I give you is light.'" (Matt. 11:28–30)

DIG DEEPER: Psalm 55:22; Isaiah 46:4; Mark 15:16–39

PRAYER: Heavenly Father, I don't want to carry all of this anymore. My back is aching, and my heart needs a break. Father, my soul is yearning for the rest only You can give. I collapse under my burdens, but today I cling to You. In Jesus's name, amen.

KINGDOM KEY: The Lord will lighten your load.

four

Made for Joy

It's as if life is a drawn-out game, and I'm just looking to make the next move. I count the days until upcoming events and look past my present. I hate that my happiness is dependent on the next thing. Why can't I just feel it all the time? Why can't I feel it now? —*the girl who hates chess*

Hey girl,

While the world chants "don't worry, be happy," the Word declares, "The joy of the Lord is your strength!" (Neh. 8:10).

And unlike happiness, you can have joy all the time; you can have it now. Happiness is temporary; joy is eternal. If all things pass away on earth, then nothing on this earth can bring us a constant state of bliss. We can find this only in Jesus, the Alpha and the Omega, the beginning and the end, the one who was and is, and is to come—the Lord who lives forever. He is the only one who can bring us joy.

In fact, that is why Christ came. He desires for us to know and prioritize our relationship with Him so that we receive the full measure of His joy. He desires to give us a joy that doesn't just fill us but overflows. It's a constant gladness that causes us to celebrate, so if you're looking toward the next party, you will always find it within you.

SCRIPTURE: "I have told you this so that my joy may be in you and that your joy may be complete." (John 15:11 NIV)

DIG DEEPER: Psalm 28:7; Philippians 4:4

PRAYER: Jesus, I thank You that You came to me and spoke life in this world so that I may have Your joy fulfilled in me. Thank you for being willing to present to me a lasting gift. May I walk in this life with Your joy as my strength when happiness is hard for me to find. May I look to You for the light that will never blow out. In Jesus's name, amen.

KINGDOM KEY: You don't have to look for more when you were made for joy.

five

You Don't Have to Hide

One afternoon I saw a meme on Instagram that showed a girl peeling off the mask of her well-done makeup and a smile in order to allow the real monster within her to breathe. It was supposed to be funny, but on a sad note, I feel this. I mean, not in the sense that I am fake but in the sense that I'm hiding what I'm struggling with. It's a little twisted humor, but I couldn't get it out of my head because the act of demasking at the end of the day reminded me—of me. *—the girl who's tired of hiding*

Hey girl,

You will not overcome any monstrous problem—or any problem at all—if you're hiding it. There is freedom in unmasking your struggles and revealing your authentic self.

Your family and friends may not understand you, but your Father in heaven does. You can't hide from Him the way you do from them; He knew you before you were formed. He knows what you're thinking no matter where you are or who you try to be in the world.

You don't have to smile and hold back tears from Him. You don't have to project a certain image. He accepts you with your flaws, your problems—He accepts your all.

Your life may feel like a mess, but you are no monster. Expose your pain, fears, and insecurities to God's revelatory and resurrecting power. Face Him and show Him your heart. Take off your mask so He can heal your hurts.

SCRIPTURE: "O Lord, you have examined my heart and know everything about me. You know when I sit down or stand up. You know my thoughts even when I'm far away." (Ps. 139:1–2)

DIG DEEPER: Ezekiel 36:26; James 4:8

PRAYER: Lord, I give in; I can't hide from You. You have a clear view of me, and I realize I've been wasting my time pretending. Today I take off my mask for You. It blows my mind that I can face You in any condition, and You will still accept me for who I am. I come to Your throne with humility, Father, as I'm ready to begin my journey of standing on Your truths. Thank you for seeing me for me and never running away. In Jesus's name, amen.

KINGDOM KEY: God accepts everything about you.

six

Take His Hand

There are so many decisions to make. At times I panic because I don't want to make the wrong one. And now my difficulty in finalizing big decisions is interfering with making the small ones. I can't handle this kind of pressure—what if all my choices lead to a dead end? —*the girl who can't make up her mind*

Hey girl,

Decision-making isn't simple, but this truth is: if you decide to become full of God's Word, it will be a lamp to your life.

Won't you allow Him to take the lead?

It's your choice—go to Him and He'll be the voice of reason you need. Yes, your own ears will hear His loving instruction. He will go with you and guide you. He will turn to you and be gracious to you whenever problems attempt to overwhelm you. He will make your steps firm when you delight in Him.

Therefore, don't be afraid to fall; He'll always be there to catch you. Life will have lots of twists and turns, but trust in God to direct you onto the right path. Throughout every slip and slide, you will be safe with Him.

Your decisions won't always be easy to make, and you will make the wrong ones at times because you're human. But as long as you seek to honor God with your life, He will not allow you to come to ruin. Instead, you will reap His reward.

SCRIPTURE: "Trust in the Lord with all your heart and lean not on your own understanding; in all your ways submit to him, and he will make your paths straight." (Prov. 3:5–6 NIV)

DIG DEEPER: Psalm 16:11; Matthew 7:13–14

PRAYER: Heavenly Father, You are my north star. You shine so brightly before me in this world of darkness that You light up my entire path. Thank you for always being so willing to show me the way to go. Thank you for being the way and the truth—and my light! Teach me how to submit my ways to You. I'd rather not rely on my own understanding—I repent for the times I do. May my feet follow Your footsteps; may I remain close to You—not turning to the right or left without Your "Go." It would be way easier to follow the world, but I choose to enter the narrow gate. I'll hold on to Your hand into eternity. Father, I choose You. In Jesus's name, amen.

KINGDOM KEY: There's no wrong decision when you are walking in God's will.

seven

Your New Beginning

I'm stuck. My past feels like home even though I know I can't return there. It hurts, but I can't stop myself from replaying the good and bad times. At least I know what to expect there. My pain welcomes me too. I do have hope for the future, but I'm well acquainted with what used to be. —*the girl who can't let go*

Hey girl,

Throughout the good and the ugly, God is teaching you how to discover the new in every day. There is beauty in it, even if it's uncomfortable. It's time to transform your perspective by forging ahead and letting go of who and where you were before. If you keep looking behind you, you will not know where you're going. You'll stunt your growth by neglecting to explore the endless possibilities with Christ.

When you do realize there is nothing back there for you, He will lead you into abundance. He will transform your desert into a life full of purpose. You will experience a new level of freedom like never before and revel at the works of His hands.

God has promised His children a new thing, and He will not be delayed . . . unless, of course, you stop Him. Hold on to His Word as you spearhead into the future together. God is bringing a freshness to your life that you can't even imagine! Are you ready for it?

SCRIPTURE: "See, I am doing a new thing! Now it springs up; do you not perceive it? I am making a way in the wilderness and streams in the wasteland." (Isa. 43:19)

DIG DEEPER: Isaiah 58:11; Jeremiah 29:11; Matthew 6:33; Romans 15:13

PRAYER: God, thank you for Your call to live right here and right now. I have been stuck reliving my best and worst moments, but I welcome revitalization in all aspects of my being. Thank you for doing a new thing in my life every day, even when I'm too blind to see it. Open my eyes and push me to live my best life with You. In Jesus's name, amen.

KINGDOM KEY: God will lead you into abundance when you open your eyes to His will.

eight

Shake Off Shame

If anyone found out who I really was, if they discovered what I did—what I still do—I would be ruined. I can't look back at my past without the memories sucking me in and sweeping me away with all the ugly that awaits me there. I can barely stand to look in my own mirror now. But to live every day where the mirrors of the world pointed back at me? I wouldn't be able to bear it. —*the girl with a history*

Hey girl,

Look to God and listen; you will not lose His love. The world may not give second chances, but He does. His grace keeps giving, and every day that you wake up is another chance for you to live in the light of His mercy.

When you decided you were going to live life with Him, He washed away the very things you are worrying about. You don't have to hide behind your weakness; you can boast in it because Christ can work miracles through it all.

So pick up your head, girl. Lay down the world that's on your shoulders, shake off the shame that dares to entangle you, and blink away the fear that's in your eyes. God does not pressure you to be perfect. His love is perfect, so you don't have to be.

SCRIPTURE: "They looked to Him and were radiant, and their faces will never be ashamed." (Ps. 34:5)

DIG DEEPER: Lamentations 3:22–23; 2 Corinthians 5:17; 12:9

PRAYER: Heavenly Father, thank you for loving me without hesitation. Thank you for being in the business of chasing my guilt, shame, and fear away. Shame has no hold on me, and I declare today, tomorrow, and as long as I live that I am a new creation. One who is radiant and unashamed. In Jesus's name, amen.

KINGDOM KEY: There's nothing you can do that'll make God love you less.

nine

He Knows Your Name

I always admired the girls in movies who carved the initials of their crushes into trees. I used to scribble in the corner of my notebook, pairing my initials with my crush's. But realistically, he didn't know my name. They rarely ever did. As I grew up, the initials went from sheets of paper to code-named texts to my best friend. It was always just wishful thinking. My crush never saw me that way—I was one of the guys or too scared or too shy.

—*the girl who never gets the guy*

Hey girl,

God knows the names of all of His creation, but He pays special attention to those He calls His children. It doesn't matter how you're feeling; He will always see you as His own.

He walks with you, talks with you. He notices wherever you are and how you're feeling. He not only reciprocates your love; His is also everlasting, unconditional, and unlike any on earth. He has written your name on the palms of His hands because you have captured His heart.

No carved tree, no secret note, no cryptic text can rival the permanency of how He feels about you. Your name is etched forever; there's no way He could ever forget about those He calls "mine."

SCRIPTURE: "I have engraved you on the palms of my hands. Your walls are always in my presence." (Isa. 49:16 GW)

DIG DEEPER: Psalms 91:14; 139:1–24; Isaiah 43:1–28; Matthew 10:30; John 10:28

PRAYER: Father, thank you for always seeing me and for loving me so much You made my name permanent. I take special comfort in knowing Your people will always be remembered. I am overjoyed that I count as one. Help me to remember that though some people I love may not find me relevant enough to consider, You are thinking of me always. In Jesus's name, amen.

KINGDOM KEY: No man and nothing can pluck your name out of God's hands.

ten

He Lives in You

Call me the queen of culture. I can recite lines from any movie, I listen to all genres of music, and my phone is filled with recent trends and updates from around the world. I pride myself in being so conscious. But sometimes after watching or listening to something I shouldn't, I feel overwhelmed. —*the girl who's culturally aware*

Hey girl,

Have you ever seen *The Lion King*? Though our culture is constantly rejecting Christ, the theme of Christ's redemption runs through many art forms. This classic movie in particular concludes that our Father lives in us. The lack of peace you experience is a reminder that He lives in you—but He wants to feel at home in your heart.

God does not expect perfection to dwell in us, but He does require us to arrange an inviting place for Him. After we accept Christ, we must confront anything that pollutes our palace— any sinful mindset or manner that gnaws away at our spiritual, physical, emotional, and mental health.

It is an honor to be in union with our Savior. When we can't see Him in our reflection, it's because we've allowed culture, instead of Christ, to fill us. But when we pursue the path to truth and abide in our Father, God draws nearer to us and we experience spiritual intimacy.

SCRIPTURE: "You realize, don't you, that you are the temple of God, and God himself is present in you? No one will get by with vandalizing God's temple, you can be sure of that. God's temple is sacred—and you, remember, are the temple." (1 Cor. 3:16–17 MSG)

DIG DEEPER: Romans 12:1–21; 1 Corinthians 3:18–23; 6:19–20

PRAYER: God, thank you for dwelling in me even in my imperfections. Teach me my limits, help me to stop indulging my flesh, and purify my heart. I am committed to making room for Your transformational presence. Thank you for the gift of the Spirit and for coming to earth and showing us Immanuel, God with us. I place You on the throne of my life. In Jesus's name, amen.

KINGDOM KEY: "Your heart is your palace with a throne only fit for the King of all kings—the only invincible, incomparable God. Protect it in preparation for your palace in heaven."[1]

1. Tarah-Lynn Saint-Elien, *Claim Your Crown* (Grand Rapids: Revell, 2020), 117.

eleven

Won't You Let Him Wipe Your Tears?

My tears are flowing freely now. I just don't see how I can get past this. Actually, I can't even see at all. These tears have blurred any form of hope that I had. I don't know what's worse: the reason I'm crying or the fact that I have no shoulder to cry on.
—*the girl who feels hopeless*

Hey girl,

No one can be there for you like God can. When King David had no one to turn to, he turned to our Father. It was the most depressing, disastrous time of his life, but he knew no matter how far he had fallen he could always call on God for an answer. God answered him then, and He will answer you now.

You can't take the heartache; you can't take the pain. But God can. He keeps track of every toss and turn as you pound your pillow in frustration. He counts every tear—the ones that make their way onto your pillow and the ones you fiercely wipe away. Let them fall; there's no need to hold them back. God is your reservoir, collecting the thundering wall of water that threatens to overtake you.

As your tears flow, He is preparing to unleash the floodgates of heaven for your miracle. He promises that you won't drown as long as you have Him.

SCRIPTURE: "You keep track of all my sorrows. You have collected all my tears in your bottle. You have recorded each one in your book." (Ps. 56:8)

DIG DEEPER: Psalms 13; 42; 43

PRAYER: Father, I'm in awe of Your heart for me. I cry—a lot. So it's amazing to think You've collected each tear after all these years. Life often makes me feel like a dam waiting to burst. At times I restrain myself; at other times I can't help but let loose. Thank you for assuring me that my tears won't overwhelm You. Thank you for wiping them away with Your love. In Jesus's name, amen.

KINGDOM KEY: You can always cry out to God; He takes note of your tears.

twelve

It's Not Supposed to Be This Way

I feel like I'm constantly pivoting; I have to make my way around one obstacle after another. There have been a ridiculous number of changes in a very short amount of time, and it makes no sense. This isn't supposed to be happening, not to me, not now—not ever. —*the girl anxious about change*

Hey girl,

When something unexpected comes our way, we're quick to say "this isn't supposed to happen"—as if we alone get the final say of how things should run, as if we're the authors of our own lives. But the truth is we're not—and that's the best part! Unpredictability reminds us we're human, and it ultimately shows us that our never-changing God is in control.

Instead of sticking to the idea of how you thought things should be, figure out what you are going to do about that change. With Christ at the forefront, we can even *be* the change! Life is so much more freeing when we release expectations and embrace what we don't know. It makes for a better testimony when we quit scrambling to figure things out on our own and simply act on faith. Our lives aren't in our hands, but we are in control of how we react.

Don't duck and dodge God's disruptions; what we do with the change determines our situation and transforms our outlook. When we try to hide from the hiccups of life, we rob God of the opportunity to show us that He works all things for our good.

SCRIPTURE: "Jesus Christ is the same yesterday and today and forever." (Heb. 13:8 NIV)

DIG DEEPER: Numbers 23:19; Psalm 102:25–27; Isaiah 40:8; James 1:17

PRAYER: Father, whenever unpredictability comes my way, I am overwhelmed and quick to wonder when normalcy will return. I completely forget that we're in this together and that good can come within change. With You, I can create a new normal. Help me to keep You in the forefront of my today and my future. In Jesus's name, amen.

KINGDOM KEY: Though life is constantly changing, our Shepherd remains the same and is always in control.

thirteen

You Didn't Have to Edit That

I spent hours editing my photo. But first I had to choose the absolute best from the hundred I took. After that, I began to edit. I cinched my waist just a wee little bit. I tucked in my stomach that was protruding above my jeans—man, I can't believe I forgot to suck it in. I brightened my eyes and blotted out the blemishes. Finally, I feel satisfied enough to post it. It's tiring but, hey, at least everything is just as it should be. —*the girl who's the Facetune queen*

Hey girl,

You've spent all that time on Facetune when God has been here, waiting for you to turn your face to Him. Hear me when I say, you are His masterpiece.

I understand social media calls for "perfection," but there's no need to spend hours attempting to attain it when God has long created you that way. As one who personally doesn't see a problem with minimal editing, I encourage you to pay attention to whether your editing is excessive, interferes with how you see yourself, and cuts into your time with our heavenly Father. That's when it becomes a real problem.

When our time is consumed with overediting, we miss out on edifying our souls. God is inviting you to find the beauty of reading His Word, speaking with Him, and pressing into His presence. Then you will take pleasure in seeking His face and not altering yours.

SCRIPTURE: "I'm asking God for one thing, only one thing: To live with him in his house my whole life long. I'll contemplate his beauty; I'll study at his feet." (Ps. 27:4 MSG)

DIG DEEPER: Isaiah 52:7; Zechariah 9:17

PRAYER: Father, I get so caught up in how I'm perceived on social media that I lose sight of Your perception of me. You have made me beautiful, but I don't always feel it. If I spent less time formulating my online persona and more time in Your Word, I'd be further along in loving myself the way You intend. Teach me how to let go of society's standard of beauty for Yours. In Jesus's name, amen.

KINGDOM KEY: Instead of editing myself for public consumption, I should edify my soul for eternity.

fourteen

Morning Glory

I resent mornings and can't muster enough energy to communicate with anyone—including God. I know they say God is the answer, but how can He be my strength if I can't seem to even reach out to Him? I'm too weary just thinking about the day ahead. —*the girl who can't get out of bed*

Hey girl,

As you awaken, get excited! God is eager to talk to you again. He wants to hear what you're looking forward to; He wants to hear your requests. Wait on Him with expectancy, and He will strengthen you. Rejoice in Him always.

Each day is an opportunity to draw nearer to your heavenly Father. It's a new day to tell the world of His glory, relive the wonders He has done, and remember His miracles. Take a few minutes to give thanks to God for the breath in your body and ask Him to guide you through the day.

This is the day He has made, and it is going to be amazing because Christ (not caffeine) will give you the strength to get through it!

SCRIPTURE: "Let the morning bring me word of your unfailing love, for I have put my trust in you. Show me the way I should go, for to you I entrust my life." (Ps. 143:8 NIV)

DIG DEEPER: 1 Chronicles 16:11; Psalms 5:3; 73:26; 90:14; Lamentations 3:22–23; Habakkuk 3:19

PRAYER: Father, forgive me for my groaning and my ungratefulness—give me Jesus! In the morning, in the afternoon, in the evening—may I rejoice in Your glorious name. You are the one true source who empowers me to conquer my day. In Jesus's name, amen.

KINGDOM KEY: God is the strength of my heart and my portion forever.

fifteen

Stop Worrying

I worry about the things I can't control (and yeah, that's a lot). I'm naturally someone who desires to feel secure—I mean, who doesn't want that? But then I'm reminded there are bills that my family can't pay, illnesses that God hasn't healed, and that one fear I always have whenever I lie in bed at night. I worry about my worries and wonder when it'll all end. —*the girl who can't stop worrying*

Hey girl,

One of my favorite passages in the Bible is Matthew 6:25–34. Jesus takes us on a journey of the creation He cares for and then says, "Therefore do not worry about tomorrow, for tomorrow will worry about itself. Each day has enough trouble of its own."

Aren't you exhausted carrying all that on your own? Do you want to live your life full of wonder instead? When we spend our todays focusing on our tomorrows, we only overwhelm ourselves and waste time. Our worrying exposes our lack of trust in God.

But when we look to the birds in the sky and the flowers in the fields, we're reminded that they don't worry about what they will eat or how they will grow; God provides, and they thrive. Our heavenly Father knows our most intricate wants and needs and will provide for us too.

Worry visits when we lose sight of God; wonder stays when we seek Him first.

SCRIPTURE: "Do not worry about your life, what you will eat or drink; or about your body, what you will wear. . . . Look at the birds of the air; they do not sow or reap or store away in barns, and yet your heavenly Father feeds them. Are you not much more valuable than they? Can any one of you by worrying add a single hour to your life?" (Matt. 6:25–27 NIV)

DIG DEEPER: Isaiah 41:10; Matthew 6:25–34; John 14:1

PRAYER: Heavenly Father, I've turned worrying into a hobby except it's not my favorite thing to do; it's just what I'm inclined to! Forgive me for not trusting You the way I should. I've wasted precious time thinking of what could be instead of living the wondrous life You have called me to. I will seek You and Your kingdom first and look forward to Your provision in my life. In Jesus's name, amen.

KINGDOM KEY: Worry visits when we lose sight of God; wonder stays when we seek Him first.

sixteen

Wild Thoughts

I overthink. It's what I'm good at. No, maybe it's what I'm best at. See? I can't even make up my mind about that! No matter what I do—or don't do—my thoughts lead me into a spiraling abyss of confusion, fear, and despair. My wild imagination leads me to worst-case scenarios and things I probably shouldn't be think-ing of. I honestly can't help it. The world tells me I can be in con-trol of my mind, but their ways to peace don't quite work for me.
—*the girl who overthinks*

Hey girl,

There is a war going on in your mind. It's one of the trickiest battlefields because it's one we can't see. It's the one place the enemy plants evil seeds and easily attacks at the most op-portune times because we're not conscious of his home base. He knows that when he keeps you in a place of confusion and stagnation, he can blindside you and win.

God can help you break the cycle. Once you first recognize that this isn't a battle you can conquer on your own, you can begin to equip yourself with His mighty weapons.

You can take every thought captive to obey Christ! How? Ephesians 6:17 tells us to put on the helmet of salvation and take the sword of the Spirit, which is the Word of God.

Today is the expiration date of your wild thoughts. Satan can't corner you when you give God control.

SCRIPTURE: "We are human, but we don't wage war as humans do. We use God's mighty weapons, not worldly weapons, to knock down the strongholds of human reasoning and to destroy false arguments. We destroy every proud obstacle that keeps people from knowing God. We capture their rebellious thoughts and teach them to obey Christ." (2 Cor. 10:3–5)

DIG DEEPER: Proverbs 4:23; Isaiah 26:3; Ephesians 6:10–18; Philippians 4:8

PRAYER: Heavenly Father, I believe I have a victorious mind in Christ Jesus—help me to surrender my mind to You. May Your loving truths eradicate every unhealthy thought and all evil that stems from it. Saturate my mind; I'll keep You at the forefront in every circumstance. In Jesus's name, amen.

KINGDOM KEY: Your thoughts have no control over you. God has given you the power to knock down every falsity with the truth of His Word.

seventeen

The World Needs You

I wish I looked like her. Walked like her, talked like her, dressed like her. I wish I drew attention like her, had it all like her. I wish I wasn't someone like me. —*the girl who'd rather be someone else*

Hey girl,

God didn't create you like her because He took pride in making you like you. He has a special mission for you, and there's no one else in the world with your design and DNA who can accomplish it in the same way.

The world needs your eyes to see His light and to show it His radical salvation. The world needs your nose to sniff out deception and to inhale the pleasing aroma of His sweet presence. The world needs your lips to spread the truth of His everlasting love and to tell the goodness of what He has done.

He created the stars in the sky. He distinguished night from day. He separated the bodies of water and differentiated the land. The Lord of all creation laid the earth on its foundation. And then, He decided the world needed you too.

SCRIPTURE: "You shall be a crown of beauty in the hand of the Lord, and a royal diadem in the hand of your God." (Isa. 62:3)

DIG DEEPER: Psalms 104:31; 147:4; Ephesians 2:10

PRAYER: Heavenly Father, to know You love every single part of me—including the very parts of me I've come to hate—brings me so much joy. To know every inch of me is purposed inspires me to stop comparing myself. Thank you, Jesus. You used Your wisdom to make every single person, every single thing. You take pleasure in all Your creation, including me. Teach me to love the way You made me. May I not look to the right or to the left but focus on the plan You have for me. Let all that I am praise You, Lord. In Jesus's name, amen.

KINGDOM KEY: You are custom-made, and there is no one on earth who can accomplish what God has commissioned you to do.

eighteen

I'm Not Satisfied

I lost it, and I want it back. I need it back. I'm not sure what that *it* is yet, but I feel like I'm missing something. God, I know You should be enough for me, but the harsh truth is I'm not there right now. What is wrong with me? —*the girl who's uprooted*

Hey girl,

Only God can ever satisfy your longing soul. Go back to the place where His wellspring of love never runs dry. He gives those who are hungry more than enough food. He gives those who are thirsty a drink that quenches like no other.

In Him, you are green with life. You are like a tree planted by streams of water that yields its fruit in season. Your leaves will not wither up and die. No, whatever you do prospers when you are His. Indeed, you are blessed when you delight in His decree and meditate on His Word day and night.

Return to Him and He will put revival in your heart. The next time you pray, tell God that you desire for Him to be enough in your life. Abundance is your portion, and you will never go without. You were always meant to flourish in His care.

SCRIPTURE: "The Lord will guide you always; he will satisfy your needs in a sun-scorched land and will strengthen your frame. You will be like a well-watered garden, like a spring whose waters never fail." (Isa. 58:11 NIV)

 DIG DEEPER: Psalms 1; 107:9

 PRAYER: Heavenly Father, take me back to the place where only You satisfy my heart. Lord, You promised to refresh my spirit and satisfy me with good things. In You, I lack nothing, and You will never withhold from me. Thank you for guiding me and giving me strength. I trust You have only the absolute best in store for me. No one and nothing will ever be enough for me. You alone are more than enough. In Jesus's name, amen.

KINGDOM KEY: Abundance is your portion.

nineteen

Are They Tripping over You?

I know I don't have it all together, but at least I don't struggle with what they do. It's my God-given duty to let people know when they are wrong, so they can be directed to the one true path. And yet it feels like they attack me when I'm just trying to help. Shouldn't they be thanking me? —*the girl "helping" others out*

Hey girl,

Heart check! Have you become a stumbling block to those hoping to get close to Christ? What about those who scoff at Him? When the world looks at you, are they seeing hate, judgment, and hypocrisy? Or are you truly mirroring who God says He is?

Our heavenly Father never holds our faults over our heads—so we must be careful not to do that to others. No one is better than the other, and no sin is greater.

It's common for us to become accidental Pharisees instead of purposed Christ followers. It's common for us to take the responsibility of punishment into our own hands. But God has called us to a real relationship with Him, not rules, regulations, and religion.

God is grieved when we push His creation away from pursuing Him. The cure for hypocrisy and judgmental behavior is His love. Here's a gentle reminder that there is no perfect Christian.

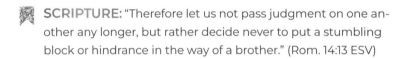 **SCRIPTURE:** "Therefore let us not pass judgment on one another any longer, but rather decide never to put a stumbling block or hindrance in the way of a brother." (Rom. 14:13 ESV)

DIG DEEPER: Matthew 7:3–5; 23; Romans 14:13–23

PRAYER: Heavenly Father, forgive me for the times I shoved someone out instead of showing them into Your kingdom. Remove the judgment, hate, and hypocrisy from my heart. You are love, and I desire to reflect that. Deliver me from me. May my growing relationship with You overrule my religious mindset. In Jesus's name, amen.

KINGDOM KEY: We must always walk in love, especially in correction.

twenty

Why Do They Have All the Fun?

This Christianity thing is becoming overrated for me. I love You, God, but I'm bored and disheartened. I am trying to live my life for You when others live recklessly. They dishonor Your name while partying and having fun, but it seems You do nothing about it. I can't imagine living my life without You, but I wish I could live a little. —*the girl who just wants to have fun*

Hey girl,

You aren't living for God; He is living through you. And you're not living a little; through Him, you have a lot. God has the power to perform miracles and greater things in your life than you or your peers could ever imagine.

He is a holy God and does not stand for some of the things the world deems acceptable, but Christianity isn't about rules and restrictions. In accepting Jesus, you have been set free.

Do not grow weary of doing good because, in due time, you will reap a great harvest. Don't envy what others are doing because, though it pleases the flesh, it hurts the spirit. Many fail to realize when you live only for yourself, that is all you will have.

You were made to live a radiantly abundant life even now. And you can enjoy many fun activities that won't hurt your relationship with Jesus. Seek Him with your whole heart and shift your perspective. The day you said yes to Him was the day your real adventure began.

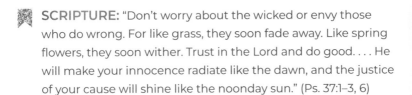 **SCRIPTURE:** "Don't worry about the wicked or envy those who do wrong. For like grass, they soon fade away. Like spring flowers, they soon wither. Trust in the Lord and do good. . . . He will make your innocence radiate like the dawn, and the justice of your cause will shine like the noonday sun." (Ps. 37:1–3, 6)

DIG DEEPER: Psalm 37; John 10:10; Galatians 6:9

PRAYER: Heavenly Father, I've been doing life with You all wrong. Forgive me for being envious of people who dishonor You. They're living for temporary treasures, but my inheritance lasts forever. Transform my heart so I don't have the desire for worldly things. I am looking forward to my adventures with You. In Jesus's name, amen.

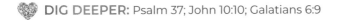 **KINGDOM KEY:** When you live for yourself, that is all you have.

twenty-one

He Calls You Beautiful

I came across an extracted segment from a highly syndicated morning show on YouTube the other day. The newscast crew was discussing a celebrity who was voted "the most beautiful woman in the world." A few went on to discuss what made her so beautiful: her thin nose, her blue eyes, and her pretty pout. They said her face was perfectly symmetrical. She is the opposite of me. *—the girl who doesn't feel beautiful*

Hey girl,

Did you know you were made in God's image? Everything beautiful flows from Him. This means all the works of His hands reflect His glory. You are the most magnificent of His creation—you are His masterpiece.

He breathed life into you. He formed the length, the width, the height of your nose. He calls you beautiful. He molded your eyes into a unique shape and filled them with colors He dreamed up. He calls you beautiful. He planned whether you'd be short or tall, knowing no matter what size you were, you'd always reach the heights of His attention. He calls you beautiful.

He filled in your skin with His favorite shades to illustrate the depth of His love, so you'd see that the praise of men and the media pale in comparison. In any hue, He calls you beautiful.

Our God is the perfection of beauty; His glory shines forth in all He has made. Therefore, you are glorious. In Christ, you are complete.

SCRIPTURE: "The Mighty One, God the Lord, speaks and summons the earth from the rising of the sun to its setting. Out of Zion, the perfection of beauty, God shines forth." (Ps. 50:1–2 ESV)

DIG DEEPER: Genesis 1:27; Psalm 139:14; Ephesians 2:10

PRAYER: Heavenly Father, I desire to be confident and completely aware of being created in Your image. It is an honor to mirror Your Majesty, so forgive me when I can't seem to bring myself to like what I see in me. I don't want to insult Your work; help me to appreciate Your creation. You didn't just throw me together, and thank you for that. Thank you for the features that make me, me. And thank you for always taking notice of me. Society doesn't have to call me beautiful; You already do. I'm fully known and deeply loved by You. In Jesus's name, amen.

KINGDOM KEY: You are the by-product of God's beauty.

twenty-two

Left on "Read"

I hate when people reach out to me just because they need a favor. If we talk on an occasional basis, then sure! But when someone randomly pops up in my phone because they want something, it agitates me. If they're reaching out only for their own gain and never checking up because they care, they shouldn't reach out at all. —*the girl who doesn't want to be bothered*

Hey girl,

I totally understand, and actually God does too. He experiences this all the time! Many people cry out in prayer only when they decide they need Him. And we have been guilty of this too. He doesn't hold it against us; He's there for us every time. But a good relationship—one that grows—requires constant communication.

Did you know prayer is the simple act of opening up to God? It's your direct line to Him—a conversation you can have anytime, anywhere, any way. You don't have to be on your knees to pray. You can speak to God when en route to school or at work or wherever. And the more you converse with Him, the more you realize His heart for you. And the more you will develop your heart for people. Use wisdom with who you decide to help, and show mercy to them in the same way God shows mercy to you.

Pray to God not only when you need something but simply because you desire to speak to Him. There is great reward when you've learned to call on God for the emergency, the exciting, and the mundane.

SCRIPTURE: "And without faith it is impossible to please him, for whoever would draw near to God must believe that he exists and that he rewards those who seek him." (Heb. 11:6 ESV)

DIG DEEPER: Isaiah 65:24; John 15:4–6; James 4:8

PRAYER: Father, I see my wrongdoing. I've been attempting to use You for what I want and then going about my day as if You don't exist. I'm like the people I just complained about, and I'm sorry. I do desire to get to know You. Thank you, Lord, for showing up even when I didn't. Forgive me for my lack of mercy toward those who would use me. I look forward to praying to You—not for what You can do for me but simply because of who You are. I know You are with me always. In Jesus's name, amen.

KINGDOM KEY: God desires to hear from you. You will reap the benefits of spending time in His presence.

twenty-three

Only God Can Judge Me

Christians are the most hypocritical and judgmental people I know. I'm tired of church people looking down at me just because I sin differently than they do. I don't care what anyone says—I don't even trust the church. Only God can judge me.
—*the girl who does what she pleases*

Hey girl,

Please be careful you don't use your comment as an excuse to do what you want. It is true that God's opinion of you matters, and, yes, He is a loving and gracious Father. However, He is also a righteous judge, and though the time has not yet come, His judgment on the world is imminent and will be swift.

He loves you so much that He has given you time again and again to avoid punishment and instead embrace eternal life. When you apologize for your mistakes, He keeps no record of your wrongs. But first you must choose Him—not the god you think will let you get away with everything and not the god hypocrites claim He is. He is the God of love.

I'm sorry the church pushed you away instead of welcoming you. I'm sorry they didn't listen to you and hurt you. We Christians are far from perfect, but seek out a church that will love you and encourage you in your relationship with God. Some of us truly do want to resemble the love of Christ.

SCRIPTURE: "God overlooks [ignorance] as long as you don't know any better—but that time is past. The unknown is now known, and he's calling for a radical life-change. He has set a day when the entire human race will be judged and everything set right. And he has already appointed the judge, confirming him before everyone by raising him from the dead." (Acts 17:30–31 MSG)

DIG DEEPER: 2 Corinthians 5

PRAYER: God, help me forgive those who didn't represent You well and forgive me for judging them with the same harshness. I desire to see You and Your people in a new light. Show me who You are and dispel every negative notion I held against You. In Jesus's name, amen.

KINGDOM KEY: "Only God can judge me" is not an excuse to do what you want.

twenty-four

Love You Like I Do

When I look to the media, all I see are #relationshipgoals. I'm not looking for the best. I'm just looking to be loved. I don't think that's too much to ask. —*the girl who wants to be someone's first choice*

Hey girl,

In the book of Genesis, you'll find the account of Leah, a young woman who was continuously compared with her sister. When Leah's earthly father and her husband looked at her, she came up short. She was always a shoo-in—for last choice.

To ease her heartache, God blessed her with what society then considered as the best gift: sons. Leah gave birth to three boys and dedicated them to her husband with high hopes of winning his heart. However, she never got the prize she thought she wanted. Finally, after God blessed her with a fourth son, Leah praised God and dedicated her son to Him. She realized the best prize was always God's love.

You see, people will let you down, but God never will. You can become bitter or you can choose what's best and pour your energy into believing in His faithfulness to you. God tended to Leah's wants and needs, and He will do the same for you. Fixing your passions on pleasing fickle people is futile; their hearts are not set up to love you the way God can.

SCRIPTURE: "You will show me the way of life, granting me the joy of your presence and the pleasures of living with you forever." (Ps. 16:11)

DIG DEEPER: Genesis 29:16–35; Philippians 4:11–12

PRAYER: Father, You fulfill me even when I feel forgotten. You love me even when I feel unappreciated. Thank you for going through all the measures necessary to show me I am Your first choice. No longer will I dedicate the blessings You give me to the hopeless chase of winning people over. I will rededicate them in honor of You. In Jesus's name, amen.

KINGDOM KEY: Fixing your passions on pleasing fickle people is futile; their hearts are not set up to love you the way God can.

Worry visits when we lose sight of God; wonder stays when we seek Him first.

twenty-five

Unanswered Prayers

People say it's foolish to pray to a God I cannot see. I feel foolish only when He doesn't answer me. I've heard there is power in prayer, but where's the power in mine? Head bowed, eyes closed . . . nothing. Head tilted, belting my heart out, and still I don't feel a thing. I'm trying to be patient, but I need a sign. It's as if my prayers ricochet off the ceiling and back into my mouth.
—*the girl who thinks God is silent*

Hey girl,

Sometimes when our prayers seem unanswered because we don't hear a clear yes or no, God is asking us to wait on Him. This may push you closer to God or pull you away from Him. But consider this: you have not been skipped over. Don't underestimate the effectiveness of your prayers because you cannot see results. And don't underestimate God because He doesn't respond in the way you would like.

Put your confidence in this: He is working. It may not look like what you expect, but I promise you our Father knows best. I know it doesn't feel like the best when you're hurting, doubtful, and confused. Let it all out; God doesn't expect you to act like everything is okay. But in these dark times, when it feels like God is silent, He still wants you to pray.

It takes crazy faith to keep speaking to God. But He assures you that if you call on Him by faith, He will always answer.

SCRIPTURE: "And this is the confidence that we have toward him, that if we ask anything according to his will he hears us." (1 John 5:14 ESV)

DIG DEEPER: Psalm 66:17–20; 1 Peter 3:12

PRAYER: Heavenly Father, give me patience. I am so tired of the wait. With my mind, I understand You know what's best for me, but oftentimes I don't feel it in my heart. I feel the weight of the wait. It's so heavy that it sometimes creates a gap for whatever I feel the answer to my prayer is. I hear Your Word, but I'm weak. Implant a supernatural faith within me. And in the process, please give me the eyes to see more clearly the works of Your hands in my life. In Jesus's name, amen.

KINGDOM KEY: Even when it feels like no progress is being made, God is moving your mountains.

twenty-six

Your Heart Speaks His Language

I just don't know what to say anymore . . . —the girl who has no words

Hey girl,

You're speechless; He knows. You're exasperated; He feels it. He hears your heavy sighs, the thoughts bouncing around in your mind. And though you can't make sense of it, He can hear your breaking heart. He not only hears it but He also is listening to it. He knows what your heart is saying.

There's no need to say a word. When the pain is too much to bear, He decodes the groans of your heart. God is here, and He has also sent His helper, the Holy Spirit, to rescue you from the hurt you feel. When you don't know what to pray, what to say, or what to ask for, the Spirit will always act on your behalf.

You may not feel it now, but you will be empowered in your weakness. God is searching your heart and will fulfill what you're longing for.

SCRIPTURE: "The Holy Spirit takes hold of us in our human frailty to empower us in our weakness. For example, at times we don't even know how to pray, or know the best things to ask for. But the Holy Spirit rises up within us to super-intercede on our behalf, pleading to God with emotional sighs too deep for words. God, the searcher of the heart, knows fully our longings, yet he also understands the desires of the Spirit, because the Holy Spirit passionately pleads before God for us, his holy ones, in perfect harmony with God's plan and our destiny." (Rom. 8:26–27 TPT)

DIG DEEPER: John 14:16–18, 26; Romans 8:16

PRAYER: Heavenly Father, I'm struggling with what to say, even now. Knowing that You understand me, that You hear me, and that You're comforting me has chased the clutter from my mind. It's been replaced with a mindset of gratitude. I just want to say thank you. I'm grateful I can be myself with You. I'm grateful I don't have to explain myself in moments when words are lost to me. I'm grateful You can empathize with my pain. Thank you for being there and for thinking of my struggles so far in advance that You sent Your Holy Spirit to comfort me. In Jesus's name, amen.

KINGDOM KEY: The Holy Spirit speaks for you when you cannot.

twenty-seven

His Very Own

They said Cinderella couldn't be a royal because she didn't deserve it. They told Tiana she couldn't be a royal because she was too poor. Belle couldn't be a royal unless she married a beast. And Meghan Markle couldn't be a royal because she was partially Black and previously married. Fairy tale or not, these women ended up royalty. I, on the other hand, have no chance of living a crowned, lavish life of riches and love. They don't need to tell me that; I already know. —*the girl who can't dream*

Hey girl,

People can and will say a whole lot, but it is God who has the final say. He has set you apart as His devoted one. He sought you out, calling you from the darkness and into His marvelous light. He created you and crowned you; He says you are royalty.

Life may attempt to lock you into a room to prohibit you from trying on your blessing. Jealousy may scream at you on all sides. And prejudice may convince you that you're a pretender. However, nothing in the world has the power to knock off your crown. You can never be disqualified when God calls you His child.

He says you are chosen and crowned, you inherit the riches of His kingdom, and you are lavishly loved. And that's all there is to say about that.

SCRIPTURE: "But you are God's chosen treasure—priests who are kings, a spiritual 'nation' set apart as God's devoted ones. He called you out of darkness to experience his marvelous light, and now he claims you as his very own. He did this so that you would broadcast his glorious wonders throughout the world." (1 Pet. 2:9 TPT)

DIG DEEPER: Psalm 84:1; Ephesians 2:1–10

PRAYER: King Jesus, Your name is the sweetest I've ever known. Thank you for chasing after me and calling me Your own. While the world may attempt to convince me to live in a peasant-like mindset, I will fix my eyes on You, King and Creator of the universe. You lift up my head, and as my head rises, my crown glimmers in Your glory. May I learn to see it and wear it every day. In Jesus's name, amen.

KINGDOM KEY: You are a daughter of the King. Nothing can take away your crown.

twenty-eight

You Have Authority

My prayers aren't like the pastors' in the pulpit. Sometimes, I mumble, and I try to muster up something to say. A lot of the times, I don't know what I'm doing. And I think it has to do with this: If God already knows what is going to happen—why, when, where, and how—why do I need to pray? Why should I pray if things are out of my control and they're going to happen anyway? Do prayers change God's mind? What power do I have to redirect the course of life? —*the girl who feels powerless*

Hey girl,

Don't underestimate the effectiveness of your prayers just because God has a plan. Don't neglect prayer because you don't see the point. The primary reason for prayer is relationship, not results. But, yes, your pleas can bring about change. There is power in prayer. There is power in *your* prayers.

Don't believe me? Allow God's Word to remind you. Hannah prayed for her baby boy, the church prayed for Peter's release from prison, Abraham prayed for Sodom, and Hezekiah prayed for long life, and God gave them what they asked for. There are testimonies around your own life that exemplify how prayers make a difference.

Yes, it is a mystery, but when you pray in faith, you unleash heaven's fury over hell. You reveal the power of God's mighty hand. You tap into the authority God has given you to trample scorpions, move mountains, and make giants fall.

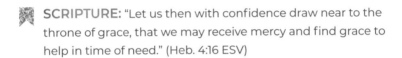 **SCRIPTURE:** "Let us then with confidence draw near to the throne of grace, that we may receive mercy and find grace to help in time of need." (Heb. 4:16 ESV)

 **DIG DEEPER:** Luke 10:19; 11:20; Colossians 1:11

PRAYER: Heavenly Father, I considered asking for confidence in prayer, but You revealed it has already been given to me. Instead, I ask You to continue to build up my faith so that I may pray with boldness. I believe You have the power to radically transform lives. Thank you for interceding for me. I am in awe of the authority You have given me so that I may find mercy and grace when I call on Your name. In Jesus's name, amen.

KINGDOM KEY: You are not a peasant; begging God for porridge will only give you crumbs. Pray with wild faith and He will present you with a feast.[2]

2. Saint-Elien, *Claim Your Crown*, see p. 40.

twenty-nine

Your Confidant

When friends or family ask me if something is wrong, I struggle whether to be an open book, share a little, or say nothing at all. It's not just a matter of trust; it's like my words decide they want to stay inside. And my thoughts? They remain trapped in my mind. I struggle to find the right way to express myself. —*the girl who can't open up*

Hey girl,

Pray for God to reveal someone you can feel safe confiding in. But with or without that person, always confide in God. There is no *right* way to do this. Just speak. God wants you to tell Him about your day and how you're feeling. He wants you to tell Him what made you laugh at school or at work and about the thing that annoyed you. He wants you to tell Him the things you typically hold back—and why.

Sure, He's a mind reader, but He would love the pleasure of conversing with you. In the Bible, God communicated clearly to His servant Moses the way one speaks to a friend. At that time, the people knew God was with them. But when Jesus came, many missed their opportunity to speak directly to God. They rejected Him instead.

Do you realize God is with you, waiting for you to speak? Or is your heart hardened to Him? You may not be able to speak to Him face-to-face, but His ear is to your heart. As with Moses, God calls you friend.

 SCRIPTURE: "Inside the Tent of Meeting, the Lord would speak to Moses face to face, as one speaks to a friend." (Exod. 33:11)

 DIG DEEPER: Hebrews 4:16

 PRAYER: Heavenly Father, please forgive me for ignoring You. I now realize You are here. I refuse to have a hardened heart. I want—no, need—to speak to You. Thank you for Your Son, Jesus Christ, who came to bridge the gap for me. Thank you, for making a way for me to open up to You. As Your own, I can approach Your throne boldly. I know to seek You for the big and small stuff. I'm relieved to know there's no perfect way to communicate with You. I'm honored I get to call You friend. In Jesus's name, amen.

 KINGDOM KEY: God wants you to tell Him everything. Nothing concerning you is trivial to Christ.

thirty

Sweet Dreams

It isn't enough that life itself is a nightmare; I have to sleep through terrors too. I'm exasperated, and for once I would like to come up for air. I've tried to escape by taking small naps during the day, but I'm not even safe there. It's one thing to have someone be there for you while you're wide awake, but when I close my eyes, I'm alone and petrified. —*the girl who can't sleep*

Hey girl,

When you face troubles, that doesn't mean God doesn't love you. When you are attacked, that doesn't mean God is not fighting for you. And when you are troubled by nightmares, that doesn't mean God can't transform them into sweet dreams.

Turn to Him before you lie down; He is there to sing you lullabies. God is stronger than your worst fears. When you wake from a nightmare, wash away the ashes of the dream with prayer and fill your mind with images of His glory. He will comfort you with His presence throughout the night. He will prove to you that neither heaven nor hell will separate you from His love.

It is God who makes you dwell in safety. You are not alone; He will cover you. You were meant to walk, talk, live, and sleep in peace.

SCRIPTURE: "I am convinced that nothing can ever separate us from God's love. Neither death nor life, neither angels nor demons, neither our fears for today nor our worries about tomorrow—not even the powers of hell can separate us from God's love. No power in the sky above or in the earth below—indeed, nothing in all creation will ever be able to separate us from the love of God that is revealed in Christ Jesus our Lord." (Rom. 8:38–39)

DIG DEEPER: Psalm 4

PRAYER: God, I know You say You're everywhere but please show up for me in a different way, right now. I'm tired of being scared. I'm tired of sleepless nights. I'm tired of this nightmare of a life. I call on You, my comforter, today, tonight, and for the rest of my life. I claim Your peace. In Jesus's name, amen.

KINGDOM KEY: Nothing can separate us from the love of God.

thirty-one

He Searched for You

I'm lost in a lot of ways. I often feel unwanted, and it's something I'm getting used to. I think it's because I've given up on the treasure of being found. I've given up on what it would feel like to be loved and cherished by the people around me. I'm in a stupor—every passing day is supposed to be an adventure, and yet they are still the same. —*the girl wandering through life*

Hey girl,

You've been misdirected, but not all is lost. I know this is strange territory, but you must put your all in God and God alone. There's no place in the world you can venture off to where He can't find you. You are His precious treasure, and He won't cast away those He chooses.

You are dear to Him. You are secure in Him. You are found in Him. He will bring vivacity in your life if you choose Him. Your wandering days will be in the past; He will fill your new days with wonder.

SCRIPTURE: "I took you from the ends of the earth, from its farthest corners I called you. I said, 'You are my servant'; I have chosen you and have not rejected you." (Isa. 41:9 NIV)

DIG DEEPER: Isaiah 62:12; Ezekiel 34:11–16; Matthew 18:12

PRAYER: Heavenly Father, thank you for finding me. You personally sought me out when I felt estranged. I am grateful You save all who are lost and that You bind up the broken and strengthen the sick. Today I believe that I am not forsaken. I am one of Your holy people. I am redeemed by You. I've gone from lost to found. You are awakening me and bringing adventure into my day even now. In Jesus's name, amen.

KINGDOM KEY: God will scour the earth to show you His love. He will switch your days of wandering to days of wonder.

thirty-two

What about Me?

I'm not the jealous type, but it's a feeling I'm sure everyone experiences here and there. I'm definitely not exempt. I try my best not to compare, but when I see the way You're blessing others and how I'm still here, I wonder, *What about me?* I'm waving my hands, trying to get Your attention. Did You conveniently just skip over me? —*the girl who's left out*

Hey girl,

God has not forgotten about you, and He will never skip over you. But when will you begin to believe Him? When will you be convinced that God is for you? When will you believe that His favor and grace are upon you even where you are now? When will you believe He won't withhold any good thing from you?

Peering over God's protection to envy other people will only bring a premature rotting to your bones. But when you look to God and what He is doing in your midst, His tranquil Spirit will settle on your life.

Don't allow a lack of connectedness with God, hard times, your own sin, or even someone else's blessing make you forget about the favor and grace God places over you. Once you accepted His Son, He let you in on this comforting truth: He will give you everything you need.

SCRIPTURE: "Since he did not spare even his own Son but gave him up for us all, won't he also give us everything else?" (Rom. 8:32)

DIG DEEPER: Proverbs 14:30

PRAYER: Heavenly Father, I am so grateful for Your favor and grace. Thank you for being the God who is for me—the one who loves me and gives me all good things based on Your goodness and not on what I believe is "good enough." If You could give up Your one and only Son for me, then I can believe You are more than willing to give me everything else. I believe You are doing amazing, incomparable things for me. You can do bigger and better when I set my sights on who You are. In Jesus's name, amen.

KINGDOM KEY: God made the ultimate sacrifice for you, and He will indeed do incomparable things on your behalf.

thirty-three

Will You Still Praise Him?

I prayed for this, wished for this, pleaded for this, and still You didn't give it to me. All of my efforts are for nothing. You don't really hear me, or if You do, You don't care. You're withholding from me, punishing me, allowing every bad thing. How are You a good God? —*the girl doubting God*

Hey girl,

The Bible shares the story of Job, a servant of God, who was blameless and upright. God rewarded Job because of his reverence for Him. Job had it all: a huge, loving family; riches; and a clear connection to God. However, Satan believed Job praised God only because of God's blessings. He asked God for permission to inflict suffering on Job, and God allowed it. Job lost almost everything, but still, with painful sores and a broken heart, he praised God.

Will you do the same? Even when it hurts, will you still love God? Will you still honor Him? Will you still praise Him?

Oftentimes it's hard to see God as good when we're suffering. But reflect on the simple fact that God won't leave you or forsake you. He is not distant. In fact, He's fighting for you. God works all things out for the good of those who love Him.

Don't praise God only if He gives you what you asked for, and don't accuse Him if His answer is no. Praise God because He is God. Job never gave up on his heavenly Father—when he had it all and when he didn't. You will always find breakthrough in posturing your heart like Job did.

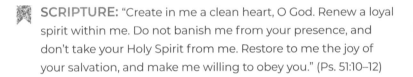 **SCRIPTURE:** "Create in me a clean heart, O God. Renew a loyal spirit within me. Do not banish me from your presence, and don't take your Holy Spirit from me. Restore to me the joy of your salvation, and make me willing to obey you." (Ps. 51:10–12)

 **DIG DEEPER:** Job 1:20–22; Romans 8:28–30

PRAYER: Father, give me a heart like Job's. I want to look at my circumstances and still praise You. I want to stand upright even when everyone is saying You let me down. I want to praise You through the pain. You alone are my help. You alone are the cure. So help me, teach me, show me how to honor You for who You are, regardless of what You give or take away. In Jesus's name, amen.

KINGDOM KEY: Worship is the answer to your woes.

thirty-four

Broken Promises

I learned a long time ago that promises are meant to be broken. I don't believe in them, and I don't make them myself. They promise they'll show up, but they don't. They promise to keep a secret, but they tell. They promise they'll stay, but they leave. It's easier to trust that people will let you down; you can avoid pain that way. —*the girl who's disillusioned*

Hey girl,

I don't believe in earthly promises, and I don't make them, either. Like you, I try to avoid letdowns. But promises are extremely important to God. You can put your hope in Him because He promises He won't hurt you.

God has many special covenants with you in mind. Open up His book and discover them; store them in your heart. The more of His covenants you learn, the more He can continue to show you that His promises aren't empty. Look at the world around you. Can't you see that whatever word God sends out always produces fruit? All that He says and does will accomplish all He wants it to. His promises prosper everywhere He sends them.

God won't ever deceive you, and He won't go back on His word. Even when people fail you, I encourage you to emulate Christ. Aim to keep a sincerity and strength God would be proud of. But remember, no matter how many times others break their promises, God will always keep His.

SCRIPTURE: "God is not a man, so he does not lie. He is not human, so he does not change his mind. Has he ever spoken and failed to act? Has he ever promised and not carried it through?" (Num. 23:19)

DIG DEEPER: 2 Corinthians 1:20; Hebrews 10:23–36; James 1:12

PRAYER: Father, I'm tired of living my life with the lens of distrust. Today I choose to trust in You. Thank you for being the promise keeper I need. I'm excited to dig into my Bible and discover all the promises You've made to me. Soften my heart to those who have deceived me and give me a forgiving spirit. May my experiences push me to be less like them and more like You. I am determined to make my word count. May my yes be yes and my no be no. I am a daughter of the promise, and I will walk in all that's in store for me. In Jesus's name, amen.

KINGDOM KEY: God will never turn His back on His promises to you.

thirty-five

Stay at His Feet

I've been so busy with my church life. On Saturday nights I prepare lesson plans for Sunday school, and on Sundays I lead worship or greet people at the door. On a good day, I don't have to minister at both services—just one. Either way, I return to church after dinner for meetings. I enjoy serving, but at the end of the day, I realize just how tired I am and how little time I have to myself. Church is beginning to feel like work—only I can't quit.
—*the girl with a busy church life*

Hey girl,

Your work ethic and your drive for excellence are admirable but don't get so lost in your to-do list—even at church—that you put time with God last. Oftentimes we think we're working for God when really we've sped past Him long ago.

We mustn't become so absorbed with what's in front of us that we forget God is here to lead. When we're so caught up in doing, our act of worship becomes less about our love for Him and more about our duty to systems. This may be your call to reprioritize. What must you cut out in order to recoup?

Serving won't always be easy, and you may have to make many sacrifices, but carving out the time to simply sit at the feet of God is worth it. Slow down and stay awhile; enjoy the peace of His presence. He is with you in your rest in the same way He is with you when you're revved up and ready to go.

SCRIPTURE: "There was such a swirl of activity around Jesus, with so many people coming and going, that they were unable to even eat a meal. So Jesus said to his disciples, 'Come, let's take a break and find a secluded place where you can rest a while.'" (Mark 6:31 TPT)

DIG DEEPER: Psalm 27:4; Matthew 6:33; Luke 10:38–42; Ephesians 1:22–23

PRAYER: Heavenly Father, forgive me for rushing past You. You are the reason I dance, I sing, I lead, I serve. May I be aware when my worship turns into work. Convict me when I'm more focused on my church life than on the cross. Slow me down and teach me how to rest in Your presence. Staying at Your feet prevails over all. In Jesus's name, amen.

KINGDOM KEY: If you are too busy for God, you are not only missing the point of ministry but also neglecting the one relationship that matters most.

thirty-six

Love Games

He's confused. He told me he loves me, but he also likes her. I just don't get it. How is that even possible? He goes back and forth between us. I can see it in his eyes: the struggle to make up his mind. With his lips, he tells me he chooses me, but I want his whole heart. I should be happy to be chosen, but it hurts to know part of him is somewhere else. Still, it's better to be loved than liked—right? —the girl who can't win the love game

Hey girl,

You deserve to be loved fully. You deserve to have a love that's constant. You deserve to have a love that repairs the pieces.

So, let him go.

Whether or not you are ever presented with one who will be able to do all that you deserve, look to God to treat you like the royal you are. Look to Him, Your King, who loves and likes you. You hold the center of His attention, and His gaze will never waver. He looks on you with total admiration, and He promises He will never change His mind. He's 100 percent committed to doting on you. Count on His love now; count on His love forever. He will show you that you are chosen first every time.

SCRIPTURE: "I have loved you with an everlasting love; therefore, I have continued to extend faithful love to you." (Jer. 31:3 CSB)

DIG DEEPER: Psalm 136:26; Isaiah 54:10; 1 John 4:16

PRAYER: Heavenly Father, thank you for loving me with an everlasting love. Thank you for Your faithfulness toward me. Though I am heartbroken over what I thought was love, I take comfort in the fact that You've made up Your mind about me. Teach me never to settle, especially in regard to how I deserve to be treasured. You chose me, and that's more than enough. In Jesus's name, amen.

KINGDOM KEY: God won't change His mind about you. He's all-in.

thirty-seven

If God Had Been There

If God had really been there, none of this would've happened.
—*the girl who's done "having faith"*

Hey girl,

You think God is way too late. You think He missed His chance to show up and show out for you. You think He blew His moment to make a miracle. Mary and Martha thought so too.

They sent word to Jesus about their brother being sick, and although He deeply loved him, He stayed where He was two extra days and His friend died. Jesus's lack of urgency didn't make sense to His disciples, but He knew Lazarus's illness would not truly end in death. When Jesus finally appeared, the sisters each said to Him, "If only you had been here, my brother would not have died."

Martha, knowing who Jesus really was, still believed God would give her whatever she asked. Jesus was led to the tomb of Lazarus, and after speaking to His Father in heaven, He woke Lazarus up.

What part of you needs to be awakened? If God has the power to resurrect a dead man, do you not believe He can breathe new life in the very areas of your life that bring you grief? Even when it seems it's over, God can create a new beginning. Step out of your grave clothes and come enter this new season He is bringing you into. He's never late. In fact, He's already here.

SCRIPTURE: "Jesus responded, 'Didn't I tell you that you would see God's glory if you believe?' So, they rolled the stone aside. . . . Then Jesus shouted, 'Lazarus, come out!' And the dead man came out." (John 11:40–44)

DIG DEEPER: Ezekiel 37:1–14; Micah 7:7; John 11

PRAYER: Jesus, You are the God of miracles! Because of You, I can believe in the impossible. You are an on-time God, and like Martha I will believe it's not too late to request help from You. I choose to believe these dry bones will come alive. I choose to believe what I experienced will not end in my downfall. I choose to believe there is a purpose and a plan for my life. Thank you for this chance to breathe again. In Jesus's name, amen.

KINGDOM KEY: The situation you're facing will not end in death. God will breathe new life into you.

thirty-eight

He's Teaching You

Why do I always have to learn things the hard way? Why do I have to learn the same lesson over and over again? Why do I always have to struggle and question and hurt? And why don't I see others experiencing what I do? —*the girl who feels like God's picking on her*

Hey girl,

Don't despise God for His discipline; don't resent Him for His rebuke. He uses discipline to draw you to Him, and He delights in you. It's what a good Father does; it is how He demonstrates His love.

God holds you to a certain standard and trusts you will handle the circumstances you've been given. He wants you to glean valuable lessons from them so you can get closer to Him. But He also uses the trials you run from to prepare you to be of help to others behind you. From these uncomfortable positions, you can pour into His kingdom. You bring honor to His name when you heed His correction.

God called on you regardless of whether or not you raised your hand. Life is a great teacher; however, He is the top educator leading you to a glorious graduation. Study with Him by your side.

SCRIPTURE: "God disciplines us for our good, in order that we may share in his holiness. No discipline seems pleasant at the time, but painful. Later on, however, it produces a harvest of righteousness and peace for those who have been trained by it." (Heb. 12:10–11 NIV)

DIG DEEPER: Hebrews 12

PRAYER: Father, I am learning that in all languages You speak love. I've sunk down in my seat and lowered my head, hoping You'd skip over me. I've avoided the hard material instead of trying to understand the knowledge and wisdom You were wanting to download into me. I'm willing to learn now. Though I may not get straight As, thank you for being by my side and rewarding me for even my smallest wins. In Jesus's name, amen.

KINGDOM KEY: God disciplines those He loves.

thirty-nine

You're an Overcomer

I'm driven by fear. I can barely stick up for myself. My shouts sound like whimpering. At times I jump at my own shadow. If life gets any tougher than what I'm experiencing now, I might as well throw in the towel. —*the girl living in fear*

Hey girl,

The devil knows that the way into your life choices is by filling your mind with his lies. Satan knows better than we do that God is greater than anything we can imagine. Satan will put on a grand play to make us fearful of him. He places strongholds in our lives, hoping we'll latch on to anything, even if he intends to use it as a weapon against us.. He shouts our insecurities and mocks us when we muster up the confidence to stand.

But Satan is a liar; he's a master pretender. He doesn't run your life. He has no rights over the children of God when Christ made a spectacle of him by overcoming the grave.

Without God you are weak, but because of Him you have immeasurable strength. Everything bows to the authority of

Christ. Because you are God's child, you can overcome anything too. Don't believe anything contrary to what God says about you.

SCRIPTURE: "I have given you authority to trample on snakes and scorpions and to overcome all the power of the enemy; nothing will harm you." (Luke 10:19 NIV)

DIG DEEPER: Colossians 2:13–15

PRAYER: God, may I walk fully aware of the authority You have given to me. Whenever I face overwhelming obstacles, remind me that I have nothing to fear because You are my Father. Be the rock I stand on when my knees buckle. Be my megaphone when my voice quivers. Today I believe in the authority You have given me. In Jesus's name, amen.

KINGDOM KEY: Everything bows to the authority of Christ. Because you are God's child, you can overcome anything too.

forty

No Prince Necessary

The world watched in awe as Meghan Markle's fairy-tale wedding came true. It was one of the most elaborate celebrations and with great reason—this moment made history. And to think it all started out with Meghan's friend introducing her to Prince Harry! Everywhere I looked on social media, I saw many pining for a prince of their own. I can't lie—I might have been one of them. *—the girl who wants a happily ever after*

Hey girl,

You don't need a prince to marry into royalty; your reign began with Christ. He is the blessed and only sovereign, King of Kings and Lord of Lords. And when you accepted Christ, you were reborn with the royal blood you now have running through your veins. He created you already complete—no prince necessary. Make the most of your singleness. Don't doubt the power God placed in you. This is your time.

As an heir to the kingdom of God, walk in the authority of who you are. Look to God for guidance as you create your own decrees. You will see generations influenced and blessed because of your obedience to King Jesus.

Sit on your throne alone. You can be impactful even in what you consider isolation. Flourish like the royal you are.

SCRIPTURE: "Yet I am always with you; you hold me by my right hand. You guide me with your counsel, and afterward you will take me into glory. Whom have I in heaven but you? And earth has nothing I desire besides you. My flesh and my heart may fail, but God is the strength of my heart and my portion forever." (Ps. 73:23–26 NIV)

DIG DEEPER: Exodus 19:5–6; 1 Kings 9:4–5

PRAYER: Heavenly Father, thank you for establishing my royal throne; I am honored to be a coheir with Christ. I want to live in Your presence and not in the pursuit of whose I can be. With a heart of integrity, I commit to accomplishing all You have set out for me to do. I will keep Your commands and remain obedient to Your voice. Everything You tell me, I will do. In Jesus's name, amen.

KINGDOM KEY: A true love's kiss doesn't give you the power to reign. Because of the blood of Christ, you can do so on your own.

forty-one

Wait on Him

This period of my life needs to just hurry up and be over with. I've tried praying, reading the Bible, and even fasting, but I haven't gotten anywhere with this situation. Everything is still the same. I am still the same hurting, miserable person. Can we just fast-forward to the good part? *—the girl tired of hurting*

Hey girl,

God understands the difficulty we have in trusting His timing. We want what we want, and we want it now. But He makes all things beautiful in His own time.

You desire to move ahead, but in this season God wants you to peer into your present. You're searching for answers because you crave security. But He wants you to see that every moment holds meaning for Him—even in the waiting.

If you choose to stay aggravated, angry, and unwilling to change you'll miss the gems that come with waiting in wisdom. While you're trying to watch His hand, you'll miss discovering the journey to developing *you*. He is teaching you something each step of the way, and He needs you to pay attention.

In this time you will begin to realize that what God has for you goes beyond what you thought was the best solution. When you wait well, He renews your strength to soar. You'll be able to view your transformation with a fresh pair of eyes. And your break-through and your blessing will be that much more beautiful.

SCRIPTURE: "But you must not forget this one thing, dear friends: A day is like a thousand years to the Lord, and a thou-sand years is like a day. The Lord isn't really being slow about his promise, as some people think. No, he is being patient for your sake. He does not want anyone to be destroyed, but wants everyone to repent." (2 Pet. 3:8–9)

DIG DEEPER: Psalm 27:14; Isaiah 40:31; Lamentations 3:25–26

PRAYER: Father, though my trust is far from perfect, I know Your timing is. My time is coming, and I refuse to let impa-tience rob me of my blessings. You're preparing me for my next season even now, and this time in my life is too vital to miss. So I choose to look to You in hopeful expectation. Thank you for reserving breakthrough for me no matter how frus-trated I get. In Jesus's name, amen.

KINGDOM KEY: Waiting well releases revelation even in the moments you deem too painful or too pointless.

forty-two

He's Not Punishing You

I'm so scared of making a mistake. Not wanting to anger God, I tiptoe through life. Like those cartoons on television, one bad move and God will send down a lightning bolt to smite me. And when punishment does come, I remind myself I deserve it. All I have to do is remember the laundry list of my failures. I think about how I can't win; I always seem to let God down with the weight of all my sins. —*the girl who deserves all the bad*

Hey girl,

I know it's easy to villainize God, but He is the complete opposite of all you're thinking. He is not a dictator. He is not a cruel judge. He is not an evil warlord. He is not an unjust king. And the more you get to know His character, the more you'll get to know His love for you.

Jesus paid the price for your sins, so you wouldn't have to. He is the only one who could. He doesn't deal with you according to your sins or repay you according to your wrongs. He is not looking down in disgust, nor is He distant.

He is for you. And His heart breaks for you when you're in pain. When life feels like punishment, tuck this truth into your heart: He is forever protecting you. So you needn't live in fear of God. No matter how many times you mess up, He will never forsake you in your weakness. He will never scare you into thinking you deserve to be attacked. Christ is your covering. Therefore, crush those eggshells you are tiptoeing upon and run freely.

SCRIPTURE: "For the Lord will never walk away from his cherished ones, nor would he forsake his chosen ones who belong to him." (Ps. 94:14 TPT)

DIG DEEPER: Psalm 86:5; Hebrews 4:16; James 2:13

PRAYER: Heavenly Father, thank you for being just that—my loving Father. I often feel that because You're the all-powerful and holy God, You want nothing to do with me. But thank you for Your Son, Jesus, who took every single one of my sins upon Himself so that I may live loved and justified. You are not against me, and I am free to live in the light of Your mercy, grace, and compassion. No more tiptoeing around and away from You. Instead, I'll run with abandon into Your arms. In Jesus's name, amen.

KINGDOM KEY: Christ is your covering; crush those eggshells and run freely.

forty-three

Armor Up

I can't stand the sight of her. No, really, I'm trying my best, but even hearing her name makes me cringe. I can count on both of my hands all the people who have hated me and done me wrong. I'm waiting on their downfall, but in the meantime, I'll try to do my best to live in peace. —*the girl who wants to fight back*

Hey girl,

I'm going to tell you something that'll permanently change the way you view those who persecute you.

But first, don't wish persecutors harm. You must heal, and they must live to see the favor and glory of the Lord upon you.

Here's the truth: they're not your real enemies. Put on your spiritual glasses; I'd like to show you something.

The war we fight isn't against those we see but against forces of darkness we don't see. The enemy will use us too if we let him. Don't allow hate or hurt to be his open door to you.

It's time to play offense and put on the full armor of God. Ask God to soften your heart and mentally equip you against anything that threatens you. Our God is a champion—good will always win!

SCRIPTURE: "Finally, be strong in the Lord and in his mighty power. Put on the full armor of God, so that you can take your stand against the devil's schemes. For our struggle is not against flesh and blood, but against the rulers, against the authorities, against the powers of this dark world and against the spiritual forces of evil in the heavenly realms." (Eph. 6:10–12)

DIG DEEPER: Ephesians 6:10–18; 1 Peter 5:8

PRAYER: God, I've been wasting my time focusing on the people who have hurt me when I have a bigger fight to tend to. Teach me how to have mercy on others the way You do on me. And show me how to fight against Satan and his camp. I'm ready to get dressed for battle. In Jesus's name, amen.

KINGDOM KEY: You are a warrior in the winning army of Christ.

forty-four

It's Okay

God loves me, so He will let things go—right? I feel horrible when I try my best and mess up on the very same things. Sometimes I wonder if there's even a point in apologizing anymore; it's only going to happen again. —*the girl wasting her breath*

Hey girl,

No child of God is perfect, and He doesn't expect you to be. Instead, He has called you to live a life of righteousness. He is the God who can't stand the sight of sin, and that is what blocks communication between God and you. But it doesn't have to be that way.

Christ is your bridge to God, and that bridge cannot break. First, He died to save you, and now He is seated at God's right hand, fighting on your behalf. Because of Him, you can go to God and He'll forgive anything, anytime, and anywhere. He will relieve you of your sin when you earnestly repent; He will cultivate righteousness as you work with Him to remove those routines that cause you to fall into sin.

If you desire a clear conscience, you can always return to Christ and confess. He will forgive you and give you rest. He won't abandon you to your mistakes—He will lead you to the cross.

SCRIPTURE: "If we confess our sins, he is faithful and just to forgive us our sins and to cleanse us from all unrighteousness." (1 John 1:9 ESV)

DIG DEEPER: Lamentations 3:22–23; Micah 7

PRAYER: God, I will forever be indebted to You for Your loving forgiveness. You don't grow exasperated with my brokenness. Thank you for Your process of renewing me and making me whole in Christ Jesus. Thank you for granting me intimacy with You through Your sacrificial Lamb. Thank you for forgiving my sins. May I learn to accept Your mercy and grace without shame. Remind me that You came to convict and not to condemn. Because Your love is better than life, I will be a living, breathing sacrifice. In Jesus's name, amen.

KINGDOM KEY: Christ came to convict, not to condemn. When we earnestly repent of our sins, He forgives us.

forty-five

Set Yourself Free

Forgiveness is something I struggle with. It's not like I intentionally keep grudges, but it's so much easier. The people who hurt me aren't worth forgiving, so I brush the offenses to the side or I bury them deep. I do whatever it takes to live my life free of the offender. —*the girl who doesn't need the drama*

Hey girl,

When you live with any form of unforgiveness, the offender still has power over you. Holding on—no matter how far removed the offense—hurts you more than it hurts them. The weight of it takes a toll on you.

Day to day, God's creation sings out in worship, but your heart has grown cold. Your lips may be moving, but God doesn't hear a thing. A bitter heart builds a wall of separation between you, but He has given you the tools to tear it down. With forgiveness in your heart, you can enter back into His presence.

God is not saying to blindly jump back into relationships with those who hurt you, but He is instructing you to let go of the offense. Jesus's disciple Peter once asked Him how many times we should forgive. Peter thought seven times was enough, but Jesus said, "Not seven times but seventy times seven!" (Matt. 18:22). Forgive until you can't keep count, and then forgive some more. God will deal with the offender.

For now, allow God to deal with your hurting heart. He doesn't just forgive and forget; He forgives and He frees.

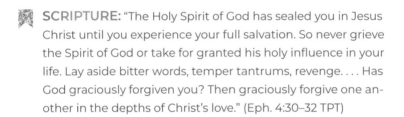 **SCRIPTURE:** "The Holy Spirit of God has sealed you in Jesus Christ until you experience your full salvation. So never grieve the Spirit of God or take for granted his holy influence in your life. Lay aside bitter words, temper tantrums, revenge. . . . Has God graciously forgiven you? Then graciously forgive one another in the depths of Christ's love." (Eph. 4:30–32 TPT)

DIG DEEPER: Proverbs 17:9; Matthew 6:14; 18:21–22; Mark 11:25

PRAYER: Father, as much as I pretend that I'm okay, I'm not. Heal my mind and give me a bigger heart. I understand what's required of me to fortify our connection. Order my steps, open my heart. I give my offenses away and recommit to You. In Jesus's name, amen.

KINGDOM KEY: God doesn't just forgive and forget; He forgives and He frees. Do the same with those who hurt you.

forty-six

He Finishes What He Starts

I get excited about so many ideas I want to implement. Sometimes I plan in advance, and sometimes I just execute. However, I start many projects and I don't always finish. I set many goals, but I struggle to accomplish them all. Maybe it's just a part of my personality and that's okay. But I don't want to be remembered for being the one who doesn't get things done. I desire to make an impact every step of the way. —*the girl bursting with ideas*

Hey girl,

Like you, I get super excited when a new idea pops into my mind! At times it can be difficult to figure out which one to start and which to hold off on, but I figured out the best way to determine where to put our efforts.

Whatever God has put on your heart—work on that first. Commit to what Christ is calling you to do, and you will always be complete in Him.

He is the Alpha and the Omega, the beginning and the end. He is the creator of all things, and He will finish what He starts. Psalm 138:8 says, "The LORD will fulfill his purpose for [you]; your steadfast love, O LORD, endures forever" (ESV). Not only that, He will not forsake the work of His hands.

You are His finest work, and you will do great things in Jesus's name. You will overcome the fear of not making progress when you align with what God has called you to do.

SCRIPTURE: "I am certain that God, who began the good work within you, will continue his work until it is finally finished on the day when Christ Jesus returns." (Phil. 1:6)

DIG DEEPER: Proverbs 13:4; 16:3; John 6:28–29; Acts 20:35

PRAYER: Heavenly Father, I believe You won't give up on me. In fact, we're just getting started! Thank you for creating me with the desire to produce. Help me to flesh out my plans so that I can completely commit to Your cause. You are the author and finisher of my faith, so I have nothing to fear. You will finish what You started with me. In Jesus's name, amen.

KINGDOM KEY: The author and finisher of our faith created you, so there's nothing to fear.

forty-seven

Like No One's Watching

I doubt that all the prancing around in church, all the hollering and bursts of excitement, is real. I believe in God; I just don't believe in those people. At least, not all of them. A lot of the hoopla is just a show, and I refuse to partake in masquerades.
—*the girl far from gullible*

Hey girl,

God isn't interested in shows either. People can make a spectacle all they want, but He is looking for truly repentant hearts excited about what He is doing. But understand there are different ways to bring the praise due His name. Though it was very uncommon for kings to do so, David danced in the presence of God—he didn't care who saw him. As the ark of the covenant was brought to Jerusalem, there was music and singing, and the people burst into praise. When the palace was complete during King Solomon's reign, the people erupted in praise, exclaiming, "[The LORD] is good! His faithful love endures forever!" (2 Chron. 5:13).

We are not show-goers, seeking to be entertained, nor are we passive spectators. We praise God for who He is, what He has done, and what He will do. We praise Him for answered prayers and for His blessings. We praise Him for turning our mourning into dancing and our sorrow into joy. We utilize our entire being—including our intellect—to give God the praise He deserves.

There will be times when the presence of God blows us away as a church, and there will be times we experience this when we are alone with Him. But He always inhabits the praise of His people. When you encounter Him for yourself, you will keep your eyes heavenward—and you will never be the same.

 SCRIPTURE: "But giving thanks is a sacrifice that truly honors me. If you keep to my path, I will reveal to you the salvation of God." (Ps. 50:23)

 DIG DEEPER: Psalm 30:11–12

 PRAYER: Father, You prescribe praise because You perceive its transformative power. I'd like to experience that. Teach me to stop looking at what others do and instead focus on my relationship with You. Thank you for the gift of Your presence; escalate my awareness of it no matter where I am. In Jesus's name, amen.

 KINGDOM KEY: God will activate your spiritual glasses when praise is in your heart.

forty-eight

Tough Love

I love God, but I'm just having a little fun. I'm sure He doesn't mind a little sin here and there; He knows my heart. And I know He will forgive me no matter what I do, where I go, and how I live my life. —*the girl living for the moment*

Hey girl,

A lack of conviction is a dangerous place to be. When you are not remorseful about what grieves God, you drift further and further away from Him. People often take advantage of His mercy, but He is no fool. He is a lamb to those who truly repent but a roaring lion to those who couldn't care less for His grace.

He desires for you to turn away from your sin so that He may save you! Real repentance is not asking Jesus to forgive you with the intent to sin again. Real repentance brings about change and brokenness. It is an honest transaction fueled by Christ's sacrifice on the cross.

Would you rather live for the moment or for eternity? He loves you unconditionally, but you must honor Him. God's children cannot live without regard for His decrees and still expect the benefits of His kingdom.

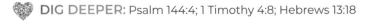

SCRIPTURE: "Do the riches of his extraordinary kindness make you take him for granted and despise him? Haven't you experienced how kind and understanding he has been to you? Don't mistake his tolerance for acceptance. Do you realize that all the wealth of his extravagant kindness is meant to melt your heart and lead you into repentance? But because of your calloused heart and refusal to change direction, you are piling up wrath for yourself in the day of wrath, when God's righteous judgment is revealed." (Rom. 2:4–5 TPT)

DIG DEEPER: Psalm 144:4; 1 Timothy 4:8; Hebrews 13:18

PRAYER: God, please forgive me! I'm sorry for taking advantage of Your mercy and grace. I thought I was getting away with my behavior, but You see and know all things. I'm so far from You, yet still You welcome me home. Thank you for loving me so deeply that You gave me this chance to get right with You. I will honor You with my life. In Jesus's name, amen.

KINGDOM KEY: You cannot live without regard for God's decrees and expect the benefits of His kingdom.

forty-nine

He Can Use That

Why me? They say everything happens for a reason, but there's no reason why that should've happened. There's absolutely no excuse. —*the girl who's bleeding*

Hey girl,

I'm sorry that happened to you. It was cruel and disheartening and was not a result of your actions. God feels the depths of the hurt and trauma you've experienced. He was there. One day you will understand that His love for you is immense and never changes. One day you will see your victory. One day you will discover that your pain is grounds for purpose. One day.

But for now, cry out to Christ. Vent your frustrations, even if He's the source of your anger. You won't always understand what He has allowed, but if you take His hand, He can transform you from victim to victor. Yes, He can use that thing.

Prayer won't change the past, but God will release the shackles of shame Satan entangled you with. God will free you from your fears and heal you from the hurt. He will birth something new through you.

SCRIPTURE: "'In the same way I will not cause pain without allowing something new to be born,' says the Lord. 'If I cause you the pain, I will not stop you from giving birth to your new nation,' says your God." (Isa. 66:9 NCV)

DIG DEEPER: Psalms 91:1–16; 147:3; 2 Corinthians 1:3–8; Revelation 21:4

PRAYER: God, I'm angry. No, I'm furious. I'm hurting, and I still feel You did this to me. But here I am; I can't go on like this. I am coming to You because You're the one option I have left. Though the past cannot be changed, show me how to trust in Your promises. Love the hurt away. Show me a glimpse of hope in this darkness. Bring new life again. In Jesus's name, amen.

KINGDOM KEY: God can use the thing we'd rather forget and transform us from victim to victor.

Slow down and stay awhile; enjoy the peace of His presence.

fifty

Thank Him in Advance

My life is at a standstill. I've been trying to open doors myself. When I finally realized I can't do it alone, I asked God—but He makes me wait. On a job. On love. On a family. On growth.
—the girl forced to wait

Hey girl,

Now can be the end of your discontent. Now can be the end of your frustration. I encourage you to develop and maintain a heart of gratitude regardless of what you're going through, regardless of what you're waiting on. You aren't forgotten. Even in your drought, the heavens will unleash a trickle of rain to remind you that your rainbow is coming.

God's doing so much for us behind the scenes that we have no idea about. But He has already done more than enough. He is enough.

This mindset—this heart of gratitude—takes time to nurture. It may feel fake at first, but the Bible says the more you seek God, the more you will find Him!

If you struggle with feeling like God isn't enough for you, start your journey by thanking Him for who He is, what He has done, and what He will do. We will miss what's ours if we focus on our needs and neglect praising and getting to know our heavenly Father.

SCRIPTURE: "Rejoice always, pray without ceasing, give thanks in all circumstances; for this is the will of God in Christ Jesus for you." (1 Thess. 5:16–18 ESV)

DIG DEEPER: Psalm 103:2; Jeremiah 29:13

PRAYER: God, put praise on my lips. Help me to speak life over my desperate situation. Give me the desire to know You better as I wait on You to act on my behalf. Thank you for all You do, what You will do. Thank you for who You are. In Jesus's name, amen.

KINGDOM KEY: A heart of gratitude brings all of God's blessings to remembrance.

fifty-one

Let Them Hate

People think I'm narrow-minded because I believe in God. They think I'm crazy because I call myself a Christian and aim to please Christ with my lifestyle. I see the stares; I hear the whispers. Sometimes people are even bold enough to discredit me in public. I can't wrap my mind around being hated for what I believe in. —*the girl who's bullied for her beliefs*

Hey girl,

If the world hates you, remember that it hated Christ first. His name alone may cause you to be persecuted. He knows it hurts when people ignore you and shut you out. He knows it hurts when they hurl insults at you and set up a smear campaign against you. He knows because it hurt Him too.

When Jesus walked the earth, He willingly took lash after lash. He sacrificed His life for the sins of the very people who spat on Him, whipped Him, and nailed Him to the cross. He even died for the people who don't yet believe in Him today. But on the third day, He rose again.

They'll try to cut you down too, but God will build you up. They don't know that the more they persecute you, the more He will shine His light over you. People may be bold enough to bash you in public, but they'll also have front-row seats as God blesses you.

SCRIPTURE: "Blessed are those who are persecuted for doing what God approves of. The kingdom of heaven belongs to them. Blessed are you when people insult you, persecute you, lie, and say all kinds of evil things about you because of me. Rejoice and be glad because you have a great reward in heaven!" (Matt. 5:10–12 GW)

DIG DEEPER: 2 Timothy 2:15; Hebrews 12:2; 1 Peter 4:12–19

PRAYER: Father, thank you for dying on the cross of Calvary for us—we don't deserve it! I have joy knowing I am saved. Nothing feels good about persecution, but I trust You, God. As they whisper lies about me, remind me of the truth of Your love. As they snarl, glare, and roll their eyes at me, help me keep my sights on You. Help me to pray for those who persecute me. In Jesus's name, amen.

KINGDOM KEY: We are blessed even when we are persecuted for our faith. The kingdom of heaven belongs to us.

fifty-two

What Are You Listening To?

Busy, busy, busy! I don't have time for myself, and my friends won't let me hear the last of it. School is a priority; work is a priority. Surely God can understand my schedule. I would like to spend more time in prayer and in Scripture, but every time I try my schedule whisks me away to another activity. At least I listen to worship music on the way to work. It's something, right?
—*the girl with a lot on her plate*

Hey girl,

You may be seeking God, but can you hear Him? Do you love His teaching, or are you just getting by? You are not serving Christ when you don't seek Him with your whole heart.

God has not called us into passivity. Your walk with Him is purposed, and even in the high speed of everyday life, His Word is the perfect way to slow you down. Meditating on Scripture is a discipline we must learn. In becoming an active listener, you gain the ability to soak in all He has for you.

When all is in disarray, you cannot rely on your knowledge to get you through the day. The noise of the world may be loud, but if you give it your undivided attention, you won't be nourished. Pay attention to what God has to say to you. When you tune out the world and tune into His voice, you can explore the facets of who He is and effectively navigate through life with Him by your side.

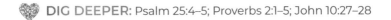 **SCRIPTURE:** "Blessed is the person who does not follow the advice of wicked people, take the path of sinners, or join the company of mockers. Rather, he delights in the teachings of the Lord and reflects on his teachings day and night. He is like a tree planted beside streams—a tree that produces fruit in season and whose leaves do not wither. He succeeds in everything he does." (Ps. 1:1–4 GW)

DIG DEEPER: Psalm 25:4–5; Proverbs 2:1–5; John 10:27–28

PRAYER: Father, forgive me for rejecting Your voice. I have put worldly knowledge over my relationship with You as if You are not the source of all wisdom. I forget that I can go about my day with You in mind. Give me an ear to hear You. In Jesus's name, amen.

KINGDOM KEY: When we are rooted in God's Word, we flourish. The noise of the world won't distract us from clearly hearing His voice.

fifty-three

But Wait, There's More

I was the girl with high hopes. Key word: was. Reality did a number on me, so what's left are empty hands. I've had moments in my life that were incomparable, and I've had gifts that reminded me of those special times. But the longer time progresses, the more I see that everything I received is eventually taken away.
—*the girl with nothing*

Hey girl,

I wish I could run over to you, grab you in a huge hug, and tell you that "better is coming!"

Have you ever seen that video in which a woman is at a ball game and the mascot gives her a teddy bear only to snatch it back and run away? He comes back with a bigger bear, lovingly places it in her arms, but then after a few seconds snatches it again! The mascot comes back one last time to give her the biggest teddy bear ever, and she finally gets to keep it.

The woman was definitely frustrated—I know I would've caught a little attitude myself! I can't help but think about how angry we get at God when He takes away His own blessing from us. Each time He proves He has something bigger for us, but each time we go through the cycle of forgetting and then remembering again.

It's hard losing something we love, but we can trust that God gives us the best gifts. As kingdom people, may we keep in mind there is always the unimaginable good when God is on our side. And may we remember that Christ as our portion will never be taken away from us.

SCRIPTURE: "But as Scripture says, 'No eye has seen, no ear has heard, and no mind has imagined the things that God has prepared for those who love him.'" (1 Cor. 2:9 GW)

DIG DEEPER: Psalms 34:10; 73:26; Proverbs 18:16; Joel 2:25; Ephesians 3:20

PRAYER: Heavenly Father, thank you for the best gift—the gift of salvation. Thank you that I am Your child and that You reserve the best for me. Show me how I can look to You when I feel as if something has been taken away from me. I believe You have the greatest gifts for me in mind. In Jesus's name, amen.

KINGDOM KEY: Christ as our portion will never be taken away from us.

fifty-four

This Is Your Opportunity

What should I do? When should I do it? How should I go about it and for how long? Wait, what if I can't even do it? You know what, I think I'll just wait for a clear sign. —*the girl who needs more details*

Hey girl,

God gave King David the blueprint for building the holy temple, and David made the preparations for it for his son, Solomon. All Solomon had to do was follow the instructions. God has also called you to follow the directions Christ gave so that you can build for the kingdom. But what He needs from you is a willing heart.

Have you ever considered the excuses given by the people God wanted to use in the Bible? Moses stuttered, Miriam gossiped, Jacob cheated, Jonah ran away, Peter had a temper, Gideon was insecure, Sarah was old. Where they found fault, God saw opportunities. God can use what we think is the worst about ourselves for what He knows is the best result.

God's qualifies those He calls. We are meant to accomplish special missions, and we are guaranteed success when we seek God despite our faults and our need to know what comes next. So be strong and courageous; do what He tells you to do the first time. Sometimes He will give you details; sometimes He won't. But He will always guide you to all He has called you to.

SCRIPTURE: "And you, Solomon my son, know the God of your father and serve him with a whole heart and with a willing mind, for the Lord searches all hearts and understands every plan and thought. If you seek him, he will be found by you, but if you forsake him, he will cast you off forever. Be careful now, for the Lord has chosen you to build a house for the sanctuary; be strong and do it." (1 Chron. 28:9–10 ESV)

DIG DEEPER: Exodus 4; 2 Corinthians 12:9

PRAYER: Father, thank you for choosing me; it is an honor to do Your will. Give me the zeal and strength to jump at every opportunity You present me. My qualifications in You are enough. May I look to You and not at what I feel I lack. I desire to work Your way. Help me just to do it. In Jesus's name, amen.

KINGDOM KEY: God can use what we think is the worst about ourselves for what He knows is the best result.

fifty-five

You're Hot, Then You're Cold

It's easier being a Christian within the four walls of church. I can sing, I can shout, I can listen to the Word, I can lift up my hands. When I leave church, it's a different story. I'm not as passionate, the volume of my voice changes, and I try not to stir things up.
—*the girl who doesn't share her faith*

Hey girl,

Many take their commitment to Christ lightly. They don't submit to being a follower of Christ. They don't choose Him entirely—they'd rather be comfortable. They party on Saturday night and praise Him on Sunday morning. They follow trends, avoid awkward conversations, and shut up when His name comes up. They're neither hot nor cold, and it's the same with you.

Lukewarm Christianity is an oxymoron. God has called you to be His representative outside of the four walls of church. Therefore, you have to make up your mind. Will you be the one who lives out loud for Him? You can't call yourself a believer if you forget your first love.

Share the love of God with the same vigor everywhere you go. Even when your mouth doesn't speak the name of Jesus, may people look to you and see the light of Christ. Be unashamed and you will see that He will make you brave.

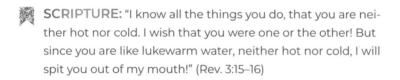

SCRIPTURE: "I know all the things you do, that you are neither hot nor cold. I wish that you were one or the other! But since you are like lukewarm water, neither hot nor cold, I will spit you out of my mouth!" (Rev. 3:15–16)

DIG DEEPER: Luke 6:46; 2 Corinthians 13:5; Revelation 2:4

PRAYER: Heavenly Father, I don't want to live like the world does; I want to live for You. Make me brave, God! Give me the courage to not only speak Your name but also live out the gospel. Forgive my complacency and show me how to shine for You wherever I place my feet. In Jesus's name, amen.

KINGDOM KEY: There's no halfway into heaven, so we must go full out in our faith.

fifty-six

Your Comforter

I haven't a clue what to say to God or to anyone, for that matter. My pain rings in my ears; my silence is enough. —*the girl with hurts louder than words*

Hey girl,

You can tell God anything—or you can say nothing at all—and He will still know what your hurt is saying. He explores our hearts. He knows exactly what to prescribe for our wounds, and He is there to help us recuperate.

Cry out the name of Jesus; He is a faithful friend. Lean on Him in times of trouble; He is a peace giver and a joy maker. Allow Him to be your comforter.

Allow God to make a way out for you. Even in your pain, He loves you and calls you to fulfill His purpose. And time and time again, every detail of your precious life is intertwined with God's perfect plan.

SCRIPTURE: "All praise to God, the Father of our Lord Jesus Christ. God is our merciful Father and the source of all comfort. He comforts us in all our troubles so that we can comfort others. When they are troubled, we will be able to give them the same comfort God has given us." (2 Cor. 1:3–4)

DIG DEEPER: Psalms 23:4; 94:19; Romans 8:26–28

PRAYER: Father, I didn't know my help was already here; thank you for sending me Your Spirit as an interpreter who empowers me in my weakness. Sometimes, I don't even know what I'm feeling, but it brings me solace to know that You are the good doctor and You know what I need. I know You are the comforter, but now I need to feel it. Become a comforter to me. In Jesus's name, amen.

KINGDOM KEY: Your groans, your sighs, and even your silence are a language God understands. Your hurting heart is heard by Him.

fifty-seven

They Will Not Get Away with It

I can't even see straight! I'm not the type to hold grudges—or at least I try not to. I know that's a sin, but Lord, help me. I try to let things go, and sometimes I truly believe I have—until something similar happens and I'm infuriated on a new level. I thought You promised to bring judgment on my enemies? — *the girl who feels trampled*

Hey girl,

In the last few years, I've undergone a series of hurts and attacks. Finally I said, "Enough is enough." My chest was tight with bitterness. While I knew the right thing to do was to forgive, my heart wouldn't allow me to release my anger.

In the book of Genesis, God tells His most faithful friend, Abraham, "I will bless those who bless you, and whoever curses you I will curse" (12:3 NIV). I kid you not—I highlighted that verse and said out loud to God, "Well, curse them then!"

It felt like God was taking forever to bring about punishment on those who hurt me, like He was allowing them to get away with their behavior. Some days it even felt like He was rewarding them for what they did. To combat these feelings, I had to learn not only to silence the enemy but also to remember this: God cannot take you where He wants to when your heart is weighed down with wrongs against you.

And so, I say to your beautiful spirit, live free and in light of what the Savior wants for you. You can begin healing only when you're able to pray for those who hurt you.

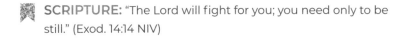

SCRIPTURE: "The Lord will fight for you; you need only to be still." (Exod. 14:14 NIV)

DIG DEEPER: Proverbs 10:12; Matthew 18:15–17; Romans 12:17–21; Ephesians 4:26–27

PRAYER: Heavenly Father, come to my rescue. Help me to release any form of hate, malice, and bitterness. I can't do it on my own. When I find myself nursing hurts, remind me I'm a sinner too. And grant me the strength to pray for those who have wronged me. In Jesus's name, amen.

KINGDOM KEY: God cannot take you where He wants to when your heart is weighed down with wrongs against you.

fifty-eight

Life's Tests

It takes me three times longer to memorize what other students get on the first try. They see the lesson and instantly understand, but I need drawn-out explanations and examples. I'm embarrassed to ask questions because that'll only reveal how incapable I am. —*the girl struggling in school*

Hey girl,

In Christ, you can do all things! Do not compare your journey to anyone else's; instead, keep your eyes on where your help comes from.

When King Solomon was newly appointed, God appeared to him, asking what he desired. Out of anything he could have in the world, Solomon asked God for wisdom and knowledge. Because of his humble request, God granted him what he asked, as well as riches and honor like never seen before.

Do not be embarrassed to ask God for something He readily has available. You too can request wisdom and knowledge, and He will give it to you. God will be your study partner, teaching you all you need to know. God will guide you toward the correct answers to life's biggest tests, and together you will reign effectively.

SCRIPTURE: "If you need wisdom, ask our generous God, and he will give it to you. He will not rebuke you for asking." (James 1:5)

DIG DEEPER: 2 Chronicles 1; Psalm 121:1–2

PRAYER: Father God, You are the source of all wisdom. From Your mouth come knowledge and understanding. As I spend time in Your Word, listening, reading, and putting it into practice, I am building a foundation on solid rock. Please help me with any test that comes my way. In Jesus's name, amen.

KINGDOM KEY: God will guide you toward the correct answers to life's biggest tests, and together you will reign effectively.

fifty-nine

His Love Chases You

I've strayed too far; there's no way I can go back now. I thought leaving would mean adventure, but the thrill never lasts. The places I venture into never feel like home, but then again, I don't even know what home feels like anymore. —*the girl who's a prodigal daughter*

Hey girl,

No place is too distant from God. It doesn't matter how far you journeyed or how long it took you to get where you are now; you can do a 180 into God's arms.

You may feel lost, but God has already found you. Like a shepherd with a hundred lambs, He left the ninety-nine for the one lost sheep. He left to pursue you. And now He wants to carry you over His shoulders back where you belong and celebrate. At first, you may approach God hesitantly, but day by day, you'll learn to accept His love with total confidence.

I don't know what you were running away from, but He wants you to know He will use your past for glory. Because you are His, nothing can disqualify you from your crown or His love.

No one can kick you off the throne He has reserved for you, nor can you give up your position of power. Our shortcomings don't shrink God's love for us. Our cringe-worthy habits don't chase away His care. His love is never ending, and His mercies endure forever. If you turn around, you will see that His love was chasing you the whole time. Your home is in Him.

SCRIPTURE: "There will be a glorious celebration in heaven over the rescue of one lost sinner who repents, comes back home, and returns to the fold—more so than for all the righteous people who never strayed away." (Luke 15:7 TPT)

DIG DEEPER: Lamentations 3:22–23; Luke 15:4–7

PRAYER: God, I've been running for so long, but today I turn around and leap into Your arms. I'm ashamed of where I've been, so it comforts me that You'll carry me on Your shoulders. Forgive me for leaving. May I find rest, joy, peace, and my true home in You. In Jesus's name, amen.

KINGDOM KEY: "You can't outrun God—His love chases after you."[3]

3. Saint-Elien, *Claim Your Crown*, 50.

sixty

Father's Day

Today is just another day. Another day of "I'll call you" but never doing so, another day of "I'll see you later," but it's been years. It's another day of strain, another day of avoiding Instagram so I don't see the world forcing family photo shoots on my feed. It's just another day when I'm reminded my dad isn't here.
—*the girl trying to make it past today*

Hey girl,

On days like these when all you're reminded of are letdowns, your mind may betray you and convince you of how unlovable you must be, based on your dad's actions or absence. This can be easy to believe when your birth father is no longer around; however, your heavenly Father is here.

Life may teach that love is temporary, but there is One who loves for eternity. God's very essence is love, and He invites you to experience His perfect peace right in this moment.

He calls you His daughter and wants to let you know that He'll never disappear from your life. You won't have to beg Him to call; He's already listening to you. You won't have to schedule a date for Him to show up; He's already there. There's nothing you can ever do to make Him leave.

Whenever you feel alone or less than, He will shower you with His steadfast love. Regardless of what you're experiencing on this earth, you're treasured by your Father in heaven. So if you thought you couldn't celebrate Father's Day this year, try again—this time, with God.

SCRIPTURE: "How precious is your steadfast love, O God! The children of mankind take refuge in the shadow of your wings." (Ps. 36:7 ESV)

DIG DEEPER: Psalm 68:5; Isaiah 64:8; 2 Corinthians 1:3–4; 6:18; Ephesians 1:3–5

PRAYER: Heavenly Father, thank you for being a father to me. Thank you for being my Dad. I've had negative experiences with my earthly one, but I'm grateful that building my relationship with You can give me reason to celebrate not only today but every day. In Jesus's name, amen.

KINGDOM KEY: God calls you His daughter and wants to let you know that He'll never disappear from your life.

sixty-one

A Seat at the Table

Whenever I enter a room, I don't think I'm welcome. I see people completely comfortable with themselves; they're laughing and sharing stories. Some even laugh at me or move away whenever I approach them. No one would miss a thing if I didn't show up at all. —*the girl who's uninvited*

Hey girl,

God has a seat at the table for you. He prepared your seat and awaits you to join Him at His feast.

At His table, there is love, joy, and His faithfulness. There is the bread of life and a cup that will never run dry. At His table, there is a refreshing calm and boldness that falls upon you. Once you take your seat, you can bask in His presence and eat without any interruption or care in the world. You don't have to scarf everything down; there is an abundance for you to enjoy.

Your enemies cannot change God's mind about the ways in which He will bless you. Your comfortability has no say. Embrace the fact that God makes room for you anyway. He prepared the table, so then take your place.

SCRIPTURE: "You prepare a table before me in the presence of my enemies. You anoint my head with oil; my cup over-flows." (Ps. 23:5 NIV)

DIG DEEPER: Psalms 16:11; 37:5–6; Zephaniah 3:17

PRAYER: Father God, thank you for preparing a place just for me. Thank you for being the bread of life and for making sure I never go thirsty. When I feel unwanted, please help me to remember that You have me in mind and have reserved my seat. I am thankful I can look forward to entering any room with You. But I am even more thankful You are leading me into rooms of splendor. In Jesus's name, amen.

KINGDOM KEY: God has a seat at the table for you.

sixty-two

Faith over Fear

Everyone's freaking out and running for cover. The shelves are empty at the supermarkets, and their food pantries are full. The news networks release troubling updates every few hours, and the presence of panic is so thick. Before I even open my front door, I am confronted with the temptation to feed on the fear.
—*the girl feeling anxious*

Hey girl,

You can either cower in the face of fear, panic, and bad news or readjust your crown and walk with Christlike confidence.

God has promised His children security, but you are robbed of His promises when you focus on your circumstances. Death, disease, and destruction are not your portion. The presence of these provides you the opportunity to live the life Christ has called you to live—fearless and unashamed.

You were not positioned here to scramble, stock up, and self-preserve. It's time to live out what you believe and spread the message of the one cure—the only perfect love that casts out all fear. What will you put your trust in? Your stuff or your Savior?

SCRIPTURE: "Peace is what I leave with you; it is my own peace that I give you. I do not give it as the world does. Do not be worried and upset; do not be afraid." (John 14:27 GNT)

DIG DEEPER: Isaiah 35:4; Matthew 6:19–21; 2 Timothy 1:7

PRAYER: Father, I give You glory for being my comfort in catastrophe. I am dedicated to fighting my fears with my faith. While others focus on increasing their earthly storehouses, I will keep my eyes on heaven. Thank you for giving me a peace that I can never run out of. Thank you for being the one I can run to. I am grateful to have Christ, the secret to life—the only life that'll last forever. In Jesus's name, amen.

KINGDOM KEY: In the face of fear, readjust your crown and walk with Christlike confidence.

sixty-three

Give with Your Whole Heart

All churches want your money. I'm hesitant to give them mine because I don't know what they'll do with it. I also must confess, I'm scared to help others because I don't have much and I'm not sure if I'll have enough for myself. —*the girl hesitant to give*

Hey girl,

While there are many causes that misuse the name of God for the sake of greed, not every organization is like that. Find a church that is trustworthy, and when you do, give your effort, your time, and your tithe and offering with your whole heart.

God is looking for a cheerful giver. He wants you to give because it shows the stance of your heart. How much do you really trust Him? How much do you really love His people? You receive what you put in. He tells us if we sow sparingly, we will reap sparingly, but if we're generous, our reward will be as well.

God also wants us to give because He shows Himself strong in our lack. Somehow, some way, He will come through for you in tax or tuition season, in promotions or joblessness.

Give with your whole heart . God doesn't want a contribution out of pity or religious duty. He doesn't reward a reluctant heart. Be like the poor widow who contributed all that she had—God wants our full trust.

SCRIPTURE: "Calling his disciples to him, Jesus said, 'Truly I tell you, this poor widow has put more into the treasury than all the others. They all gave out of their wealth; but she, out of her poverty, put in everything—all she had to live on.'" (Mark 12:43–44 NIV)

DIG DEEPER: Mark 12:41–44; 2 Corinthians 9:6–15

PRAYER: Father, forgive me for my greed. I don't want to make excuses. Everything I have is because of You. Even when I have nothing, I have something, for You have made me rich in You. May I be a good steward of Your money by paying my tithes and giving when You lead me to. In Jesus's name, amen.

KINGDOM KEY: Even when you have nothing, you have something—God has made you rich in Him.

sixty-four

The Breakdown

I don't regret the mess. The people. The situations. The hurt I feel. I've lost my footing and I'm heartbroken, but I understand this pain is the basis for where I am about to be. It's just hard to see right now. —*the girl at rock bottom*

Hey girl,

One thing I've learned is that we are not "all good" until we let God in on every single thing that inhabits our space. I thought I was giving God every piece of me until He showed me there was still a little bit left to hand over. In my case, He had to take it Himself, forcing me to look at my empty hands. In that time of brokenness, I learned to turn my hands upward. Because when we are stripped of everything, we are quick to cling to God.

In the life of David, he lost everything that made him "all good": his popularity, wife, mentor, best friend, country, and finally, his dignity—all in ten years. But he gained total dependence on the only God who promises us great things.

God loves us but He cannot work extraordinarily with one who refuses to bend and break. When we close off our hearts in pride, He will continually chip away at our hardness. Sometimes it's gradual and sometimes it's all at once. But He uses difficult times to draw us near to Him.

He is close to the brokenhearted. When we are crushed, He saves us. In the crushing, in the breaking, God is remolding us. May we be willing clay in our Potter's hands.

SCRIPTURE: "He humbled you, and in your hunger He gave you manna to eat, which neither you nor your fathers had known, so that you might understand that man does not live on bread alone, but on every word that comes from the mouth of the Lord." (Deut. 8:3 BSB)

DIG DEEPER: Psalm 34:18

PRAYER: Lord, forgive me, for I've been so prideful, putting my security in blessings You have given me. I know You to be gracious. You are not breaking me to hurt me; You are breaking me to build me up in You. Thank you that even at rock bottom, I can look up. May I not resist the works of Your hands but embrace being molded by You. In Jesus's name, amen.

KINGDOM KEY: Through our hardship, God is remolding us. May we be willing clay in our Potter's hands.

sixty-five

The Same Page

I'm not keen on surprises. I enjoy being the ruler of my space and feeling safe in the knowledge of what's to come. Of course, in this digital age, things change rapidly online, further influencing our already hectic world. Whether it's an unexpected loss, an election, or a natural disaster, any surprise is really just an ambush. —*the girl who doesn't like surprises*

Hey girl,

When we step up to the plate, seeking out the plans of God prior to picking up our planners, we won't strike out. Unlike this uncertain generation, God is constant, and nothing is a surprise to Him. He is independent of all things that exist. He is the same yesterday, today, and forever. No created thing is as stable and permanent as the Creator of the universe.

Though changes in our world are occurring at an alarming rate, the Word of God gave us a heads-up two thousand years ago. There will be things we don't understand, but the Bible invites us to be on the same page with the all-knowing God. We enter a place of peace by listening to His voice.

Regardless of the year, the day, or the moment, we don't have to refigure out who Jesus is or where He stands. Life may throw us curveballs, but God is at bat, bringing our team to our forever home run.

SCRIPTURE: "God, it seems you've been our home for-ever; long before the mountains were born. Long before you brought earth itself to birth, from 'once upon a time' to 'king-dom come'—you are God." (Ps. 90:1–2 MSG)

DIG DEEPER: Deuteronomy 32:4; Psalms 20:7–8; 62:2; Matthew 7:24–27

PRAYER: God, You were before all things, You are in all things, and You will be after all things. Thank you that You remain the same and You know what's coming. The world is moving further away from You, but at this moment, I draw near to You and declare that You are the rock on which I stand. In Jesus's name, amen.

KINGDOM KEY: "Nothing can catch God by surprise because He knows the past, present, and future. He lives in eternity and is waiting for us there."[4]

4. Saint-Elien, *Claim Your Crown*, 27–28.

sixty-six

Get Out of Your Comfort Zone

Did I just hear You correctly? People think I'm out of touch to believe in a God I cannot see. They think it's crazy that I speak to You, and they think it's even crazier that I believe I get a response. Isn't trusting You enough, God? Are You really telling me to take this faith journey a step further into the deep end?
—*the girl who needs to make sure*

Hey girl,

When you accepted Christ as your Savior, you agreed to give Him full access. When He is calling you, don't close yourself off. When He says go there, don't glue your feet to your box.

People thought it was crazy when God instructed Noah to build an ark—until it began to rain. They thought it was crazy when a lame man was lowered through a roof for healing—until he picked up his mat and walked. Therefore, stand, even if your knees buckle. Speak, even if your voice shakes. Seek God, even when the world tells you He's nowhere to be found.

As we journey through this life together, keep this in mind: the thoughts and beliefs of the doubters are temporary. One day every knee will bow and every tongue will confess that He is Lord. It won't be so crazy then.

SCRIPTURE: "If it seems we are crazy, it is to bring glory to God. And if we are in our right minds, it is for your benefit. Either way, Christ's love controls us. Since we believe that Christ died for all, we also believe that we have all died to our old life. He died for everyone so that those who receive his new life will no longer live for themselves. Instead, they will live for Christ, who died and was raised for them." (2 Cor. 5:13–15)

DIG DEEPER: Galatians 2:20; 6:7; 2 Peter 1:3–11

PRAYER: Father, Your sacrifice is reason enough to live out a life that best represents You. You did not call me to cower in my seat but to stand courageously, even in situations that may seem crazy. I am willing to be used in any way so that those who see me may see You. In Jesus's name, amen.

KINGDOM KEY: I will stand courageously and not cower in whatever situations God calls me to.

sixty-seven

A Change of Heart

How can I be sinful if I'm a good person? I'm happiest when I see people doing well , and if someone is suffering, I will do anything in my power to help. I know I'm not perfect, but I do care.
—*the girl with a good heart*

Hey girl,

A heart softened toward the needs of people is beautiful, but does your heart break for what hurts God's heart? Oftentimes, we're led to believe that being good is good enough, but "good" won't get us inside the gates of heaven. Accepting the Son of God will; loving Him more each day will.

Born into sin, we naturally have hearts of stone. The stony heart is one that isn't willing to change and is aloof to the things of God. But when we are born again, Jesus softens and transforms it into a heart of flesh.

This new heart has a sincere sensitivity toward sin and grieves over offenses against our Father. It yields to His nudges and pursues His will. It is an undivided heart, one that pledges allegiance to the one true King.

SCRIPTURE: "I will give you a new heart, and I will put a new spirit in you; I will take out your stony, stubborn heart and give you a tender, responsive heart." (Ezek. 36:26)

DIG DEEPER: Romans 5:12–21; 1 John 1:10

PRAYER: Father, You honor goodness, but You honor a heart after Yours first and foremost. Wherever You see hardness in me, please chip away at it. Whenever I resist You in any way, show me. Whenever I fail to listen, speak louder. I do not have the power to make a pliable, soft heart. It is a precious gift from You that I desperately need. In Jesus's name, amen.

KINGDOM KEY: Christ can heal your heart from its hardness. He's willing to give you a new heart and a new spirit.

sixty-eight

Let It All Out

I pride myself on being tough; I can honestly count the few times I've cried in years on one hand! Being emotional is a weakness to me. —*the girl out of touch with her feelings*

Hey girl,

After a pruning season full of unanswered prayers, hurts, and betrayals, I was forced to embrace my feelings. Sometimes I'd find tears in my eyes seemingly out of nowhere! I would tell myself to get it together because it was so unlike me, but that didn't stop it from happening again.

The first time my eyes betrayed me in public, I was invited to share my story at an intimate women's event. We were sitting in a circle, going around and answering questions we'd pulled from a jar. My question was, How do you deal with stress? At first I expressed that I never know when I am stressed—typically those closest to me will tell me. Then the tears started, and all I planned to say completely flew out the window.

I was shocked to feel those tears slide down my face, defying my efforts to stop them. As I tried to compose myself, the women insisted I let the tears fall. They insisted I not apologize for them. They insisted that I needed this. And that they did too.

God pressed for a more vulnerable, less structured me so that a release could take place. I thought my doing it in private was enough, but there is much liberation in sharing the moment with those who will pray for you and love on you. Find your safe haven and do just that.

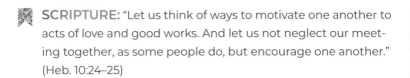 **SCRIPTURE:** "Let us think of ways to motivate one another to acts of love and good works. And let us not neglect our meeting together, as some people do, but encourage one another." (Heb. 10:24–25)

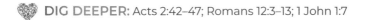 **DIG DEEPER:** Acts 2:42–47; Romans 12:3–13; 1 John 1:7

PRAYER: Father, where I am weak, You are strong. May I learn to embrace every season I am in and bring all my cares to You first. There is nothing embarrassing about what You are doing in my life. Teach me how to turn to a friend to help ease my burden instead of fighting my feelings. In Jesus's name, amen.

KINGDOM KEY: It's important to have someone who will let you feel what you feel and who will pour into you as you pour out.

sixty-nine

The World Is Waiting

It's taken me a while to be proud of where I am, but now that I'm here, I'm not satisfied. Don't get me wrong—I'm in a place where all my desires are pushed to the side and I can clearly sense God calling me to act. So I'm excited! I feel something bubbling inside of me. But I don't know what's next. *—the girl who's waiting to act*

Hey girl,

There are times in our lives when we're trying to allow everything to sink in, and as we're processing, we feel a strong push. We feel a push to do something big—something that will cause a ripple effect through our circles and across borders.

Maybe you've been feeling that too. I don't know what you've been working on or what you've been thinking about creating, but I'm here to tell you that your time is now. Do it *now.*

There is a call over all of our lives, and if we don't take heed—if we are not sensitive to the seasons we're in—we'll be waiting forever for that one thing to come to fruition. You may say you're waiting on this or that, but quite frankly, the world is waiting on you!

What can you do for the kingdom? How will you show the world God's glory? Your time is now!

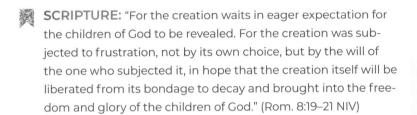

SCRIPTURE: "For the creation waits in eager expectation for the children of God to be revealed. For the creation was subjected to frustration, not by its own choice, but by the will of the one who subjected it, in hope that the creation itself will be liberated from its bondage to decay and brought into the freedom and glory of the children of God." (Rom. 8:19–21 NIV)

DIG DEEPER: Romans 8:15; Ephesians 6:18–20; Philippians 1:20; Philemon 1:4–7

PRAYER: God, I don't want to be the one holding You up. I don't want to be the one who misses Your moment. Father, may I be so in tune with You that I am attentive to where You want me to go, what You want me to say, and what You want me to do. I desire to find true contentment in doing what You have called me to. Bring revival so that the world may see You in me. In Jesus's name, amen.

KINGDOM KEY: The world is waiting on you to display God's glory.

seventy

Do You Remember?

Instagram is the first app I check when I wake up—I can't help it. Next thing I know, I'm scrolling and laughing at TikTok for an hour. I downloaded the Bible app a long time ago, but it's buried somewhere in one of my folders. I know I should spend more time with God, but at least I've told Him "good morning."
—*the girl who scrolls past the Bible app*

Hey girl,

Whenever I feel like doing other things instead of digging into the Word of God, I think of those who must hide out in order to have church and of those who have only scraps of the New Testament in their pockets. I think of those who don't have Bibles at all and of those who cry with joy when gifted with one.

When was the last time God's Word moved you? When was the last time you sat at His feet, eager to learn what He had to tell you? Like the church in Ephesus, have you been acting like a Christ follower but rejecting your first love (Rev. 2:2–7)?

With so many things vying for our attention, it's quite easy to begin taking God for granted. We allow distractions to fill up our time and give God the leftovers. But we can't do the bare necessities to claim we have God on our side when really we left Him long ago.

Make God your priority—anything we choose before Him is an idol. God will never force us to seek His presence; it's our choice. But the best option will always be to pick up our cross—before we pick up our phones—and follow Him.

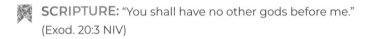 **SCRIPTURE:** "You shall have no other gods before me." (Exod. 20:3 NIV)

 **DIG DEEPER:** Matthew 10:38–39; John 3:30; Romans 8:5

PRAYER: Father, I remember now. You are the one true God! Forgive me for falling away and giving You only scraps of my time. Help me to become more disciplined. Thank you for convicting me and welcoming me back into Your arms as You take Your rightful place on the throne of my heart. I don't want to just spend time with You; I want to spend time with You *first*. In Jesus's name, amen.

KINGDOM KEY: Your phone may be an extension of you but make God your priority. He lives in you.

seventy-one

He Hasn't Let You Down

Well, I'm all out of options now. I've tried everything with God—He has been my one and only plan. I don't ask for much, but I really thought He would help me out with this one. Why couldn't He just come to my rescue when I needed Him the most? —*the girl who can't fight anymore*

Hey girl,

I understand you're feeling stuck right now. You may be thinking that God has some way of showing up for you, huh? With eyes wide open, you waited on Him in expectation, but as time went on, the light began to dim. You cried. You screamed. But still, through it all, you had a little hope that things would work out.

What if I told you that they will? What if you hold on a little longer? What if you said right now, "God is able"?

When you hold God as your first resort, He will always honor you. He will fight for you and lead you to victory. The victories God leads you to won't always look like how you envisioned them, but He will strengthen you and show you what to do. He will move mountains on your behalf.

Don't let that little mustard seed of faith die. Plant it in your heart; water it with your tears. One day soon you will flourish in your faith. You will quickly see that you can overcome anything with God as your commander in chief.

You will celebrate your wins in Christ; He can do all things but fail! He has never lost a single battle, and He won't begin with you.

SCRIPTURE: "Thanks be to God, who in Christ always leads us in triumphal procession, and through us spreads the fragrance of the knowledge of him everywhere." (2 Cor. 2:14 ESV)

DIG DEEPER: Matthew 13:31–32; 17:20; 1 Corinthians 15:57; Hebrews 11:1

PRAYER: Heavenly Father, I thought You let me down, and to be honest, I still feel You did. But I'm fighting with my little mustard seed of faith. I'm fighting because deep down inside of me I know there's no plan B I can turn to in my life. Nothing is impossible for You; I know You will make a way for me. Thank you for being the champion of my story. In Jesus's name, amen.

KINGDOM KEY: You will celebrate your wins in Christ. God has never lost a single battle, and He won't begin with you.

seventy-two

Applause

We live in a society where we're told to pat ourselves on the back for every single thing. At times this is translated into the church with people who make a grand display of helping those less fortunate. I can't lie—it does feel pretty good to be commended for all I do. —*the girl who loves getting the credit*

Hey girl,

There will be accomplishments in your life that the world can't ignore. God will elevate you for all to see. However, when it comes to the assignments He has given you, don't complete them with your own glory in mind. For if you do, that is all the reward you will receive.

God did not give you your life to impress people. Your mission is not complete when society is satisfied with your accomplishments; your mission is complete when you fulfill the purpose God created you for.

Is it enough for you to know that He is proud of you? Is it enough to know that heaven applauds anything you do for His glory? Do you live for temporary applause on earth or would you rather our heavenly Father welcome you into eternity saying, "Well done"?

SCRIPTURE: "Watch out! Don't do your good deeds publicly, to be admired by others, for you will lose the reward from your Father in heaven. When you give to someone in need, don't do as the hypocrites do—blowing trumpets in the synagogues and streets to call attention to their acts of charity! I tell you the truth, they have received all the reward they will ever get. But when you give to someone in need, don't let your left hand know what your right hand is doing. Give your gifts in private, and your Father, who sees everything, will reward you." (Matt. 6:1–4)

DIG DEEPER: Psalms 19:14; 147:1–11; 1 Thessalonians 2:4; Hebrews 13:16

PRAYER: Jesus, humble me. It's easy to get caught up by the compliments of those around me, but in doing so, I puff up my chest and push myself away from Your approval. May I seek the applause of One; may I seek You. Thank you for all You have done through my life and what You will continue to do. Help me to remember to redirect all the credit and glory and honor to Your name. In Jesus's name, amen.

KINGDOM KEY: True reward is hearing the words "well done" and being welcomed into eternity.

seventy-three

The Lord Remembers You

Disney inspires us to wish upon a star, and the younger, wistful me used to. I would look out my window, tilt my head up, squeeze my eyes shut, and murmur my deepest desire. Clearly, that doesn't work, but neither does prayer. I don't see much of a point in speaking to God; He never gives me what I want anyway. —*the girl who's done asking*

Hey girl,

The Lord remembers you. That is the biblical promise Hannah remembered when God finally granted her deepest desire, a baby boy. It took years of tears, desperation, and persecution. But she was persistent; she prayed with her whole heart.

He wants your whole heart too. God wants you to approach Him not just with your requests but for a relationship. Ask Him to help your unbelief because, yes, He does respond.

God is not a genie, but He does want to gift His children. There are already many gifts we aren't yet aware of. We don't know what He has promised because we don't know His voice.

As we wait for the way in which God will answer us, we must immerse ourselves in His living, breathing Word. We won't always get what we're asking for, but when we squeeze our eyes shut and kneel before our Father, we will be comforted that our prayers don't fly up to space. Our prayers go out to a Friend with never-ending mercy, compassion, and grace. He will give us what's right for us because He is the Father who knows best.

SCRIPTURE: "But as for me, I watch in hope for the Lord, I wait for God my Savior; my God will hear me." (Micah 7:7 NIV)

DIG DEEPER: 1 Samuel 1; Psalm 66:17–20; 1 Peter 3:12

PRAYER: God, forgive me for approaching You like a vending machine. My time, my attention—show me how to devote them to You. As I'm awaiting Your answer to my requests, reveal what You have promised me in Your Word. I pray I begin to desire things that bring You glory. Show me when my asks align with Your will. May I desperately seek You as Hannah did and accept whatever Your final answer may be. In Jesus's name, amen.

KINGDOM KEY: "We can wish upon a star all we want, or we can pray to the star-breather, the One who created them. Wishes go unanswered, but our prayers will always be heard by God."[5]

5. Saint-Elien, *Claim Your Crown*, 86.

seventy-four

The Star of the Show

Not even one "thank you," but that's to be expected . . . I mean, is expressing appreciation really that hard to do? Just because I'm not in the limelight doesn't mean I don't deserve any acknowledgment. —*the girl tired of being underappreciated*

Hey girl,

In all stages of life, God's eyes are on you. When people attempt to take you for granted, trust that as you are doing what God has assigned you, He gets the glory and He gifts you for your faithfulness.

It's unhealthy to stay somewhere you are not appreciated, but do understand there will be times God assigns you a role you may not like. This is one way He develops your character.

You can make your big debut by stepping into who He has called you to be—no matter where you are onstage. You have an audience of one, and He is looking down with a megaphone and streamers, cheering you on.

God takes the lead when we play the background. As you walk in your calling, redirect the spotlight to Him and allow the world to see God in you. In the end, He gets the standing ovation.

SCRIPTURE: "They sang, 'Amen! Blessing and glory and wisdom and thanksgiving and honor and power and strength belong to our God forever and ever! Amen.'" (Rev. 7:12)

DIG DEEPER: Psalms 8:4; 138:8; Isaiah 49:15; Matthew 10:30–31

PRAYER: God, show me how to deal with those who overlook me, and help me to be satisfied with being the apple of Your eye. May I give You glory through my lifestyle even when I'm in a place I don't want to be. Thank you for not only being mindful of me but also simply appreciating who I am. I will redirect all glory and honor and praise to You. In Jesus's name, amen.

KINGDOM KEY: God takes the lead when we play the background.

Christ as our portion will never be taken away from us.

seventy-five

Mondays

Here we go again. After an amazingly sloth-ish weekend, it's time to mentally prepare for the week ahead. I'm already exhausted just thinking about classes and work. Feelings of anxiousness rise to new heights when I think of the pressure to show up and follow orders over and over again. Mondays are the worst. —*the girl who's over it already*

Hey girl,

Weekdays can be very overwhelming, but looking forward to Friday shouldn't be the only thing that gets us through them. I've begun to appreciate Monday because it is not only the start of something new but also another day the Lord has called us to serve Him with all of our hearts.

When we drag our feet, when we keep our eyes on the clock and halfheartedly do an assignment, when we slack off once our bosses and professors turn their backs, we aren't "getting away" with anything. In fact, we are cheating ourselves. It may be hard to see, but the work you do now is training ground for the ultimate work God has called you to.

Whether you hate where you are or not, you aren't working for man. You're working to please your heavenly Father. He has the ultimate rewards, and He holds all the bonuses and benefits you need. He will satisfy you with the joy of His presence forever.

Now, put your heart into it and get to work!

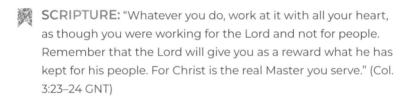 **SCRIPTURE:** "Whatever you do, work at it with all your heart, as though you were working for the Lord and not for people. Remember that the Lord will give you as a reward what he has kept for his people. For Christ is the real Master you serve." (Col. 3:23–24 GNT)

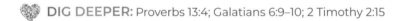 **DIG DEEPER:** Proverbs 13:4; Galatians 6:9–10; 2 Timothy 2:15

PRAYER: Dear God, nudge me whenever I complain so that I'm reminded to work heartily no matter where I am. Humble me, Father, and purify my motives. Help me to keep my eyes on You and not on the clock. Your reward is the only motivation I need to obey. In Jesus's name, amen.

KINGDOM KEY: Keep your eyes on Christ, not on the clock. Fulfill your duties with receiving His bonuses in mind.

seventy-six

All I Have to Give

The gratitude I feel toward God is overwhelming! I can't believe I'm forgiven; I can't believe He loves me for me. It makes me want to shout and dance, and sometimes I scramble, looking for something—anything—to give back to Him. —*the girl in awe*

Hey girl,

In Scripture, Mary Magdalene goes down in history as a woman who gave with her whole heart. After being forgiven and transformed from her former lifestyle, her refreshed heart was filled with adoration for her Savior. Her praise propelled her to pour out expensive perfume, anointing Jesus's head and feet. She was chastised for being wasteful, but Jesus honored her. He knew Mary spilled out all she had to give because she believed He was worth it.

And He was, and He is.

Your posture of praise pleases the Lord. There's nothing in the world you could gift God as repayment for His loving-kindness. However, dedicating your life as a living sacrifice to Him rises to His throne as sweet perfume.

When you live your life in thankful dedication to your Savior, He then spreads a fragrance everywhere you go. Like Mary's sweet sacrifice that we so often speak of today, it is a lasting perfume.

Bring Him your every breath, your everything. As you continually offer up a sacrifice of praise to God and acknowledge His name, He will give abundant life.

SCRIPTURE: "Beloved friends, what should be our proper response to God's marvelous mercies? I encourage you to surrender yourselves to God to be his sacred, living sacrifices. And live in holiness, experiencing all that delights his heart. For this becomes your genuine expression of worship." (Rom. 12:1 TPT)

DIG DEEPER: John 12:1–8; 2 Corinthians 2:14–16

PRAYER: Father, every day I will give You my time, my listening ear, my things, my ambitions, my everything—I rededicate them right back to You. There's nothing I will refuse You. As my praises rise and I enter Your presence, I pray You smell honor. Fill my life completely, so that I may fill the world with You. Delight in me, Lord. May You get the glory through me. In Jesus's name, amen.

KINGDOM KEY: God enjoys the unmistakable aroma of our lifestyle of worship.

seventy-seven

The Finish Line

I'm so frustrated. I work hard, but it's like life is a treadmill and I'm seeing the same surroundings. I'm running in place. I feel the pressure to keep up the pace or go even faster. I can't afford to mess up; there's too much on the line. One little slipup and I feel like I'll be back at square one. —*the girl who doesn't want to start over*

Hey girl,

The first time I completed an obstacle course, I *loved* it. We were several feet in the air, secured only by a harness and a cable, yet I was in my element. I leaped, I ran, I crawled. When the course got difficult, the guide yelled, "Don't look down!" But I didn't fear looking down; I feared losing my place. Being able to see the finish line helped; I kept pushing even with the cable yanking me backward.

You can do this too. Keep your eyes on Christ, and He will give you grace and sustenance when you're running out of fuel. He will track your progress and help you stay at a steady pace. With Him, you don't lose time—you gain momentum.

Even when you are knocked down, you won't be destroyed. There will always be a next step. Run with victory in mind. With every step and every leaped obstacle, you will gain perseverance and a better outlook on your situation.

SCRIPTURE: "I admit that I haven't yet acquired the absolute fullness that I'm pursuing, but I run with passion into his abundance so that I may reach the purpose that Jesus Christ has called me to fulfill and wants me to discover. I don't depend on my own strength to accomplish this; however, I do have one compelling focus: I forget all of the past as I fasten my heart to the future instead." (Phil. 3:12–13 TPT)

DIG DEEPER: Philippians 3

PRAYER: Father God, thank you for being my pacemaker. Thank you for being the breath of fresh air I so desperately need. I pray for endurance and peace when I stumble. May I always get back up, letting go of my past and the expectations I set for myself as I press on toward the mark for which You've called me. In Jesus's name, amen.

KINGDOM KEY: Face whatever you're experiencing head-on. Keep moving forward. God will give you the strength to make it to the other side.

seventy-eight

Don't Let Them Cut Off Your Sound

It seems I'm never at a loss for words—well, at least in my mind. Thoughts fly through a mile a minute, but oftentimes what I'd like to say gets lodged in my throat. They don't have to shut me up; sometimes I do it for them. —*the girl who struggles to speak up*

Hey girl,

After a full day of editing my YouTube video, "25 Biblical Affirmations That'll Build Your Confidence and Transform Your Life," the audio stopped. Thinking it was a mistake, I kept dragging my cursor back to the spot where the silence began, but there was indeed a glitch. The audio cut off right as I was saying, "No matter what I go through, God's glory will be revealed through my life."

I didn't know how I was going to finish my project, and I almost let discouragement win until I remembered something —of course, the enemy will try to cut off our sound! I don't think it was an accident that the audio stopped where it did.

Satan will always attempt to cut off our memory and any advances we make for God's kingdom. He doesn't want us making biblical affirmations; he wants us to struggle in our identities. He knows that when we are stuck, we are silenced.

The enemy doesn't want you to know who you are, but I am here to tell you of the impact your life can have. You are more than a conqueror, and your royal authority comes from King Jesus. When you position yourself in Christ, you can speak life with all your being. Your voice matters; don't allow anyone—not even yourself—to muzzle your message.

SCRIPTURE: "The tongue has the power of life and death, and those who love it will eat its fruit." (Prov. 18:21 NIV)

DIG DEEPER: Psalm 30:1; Jeremiah 1:9; Acts 18:9–10; 1 Peter 3:15–16

PRAYER: Heavenly Father, remind me of who I am and give me the confidence to speak up with purpose. I realize the power of my voice and know the promises You made to me; I claim them over my life. I refuse to let any form of negativity prosper. Help me to speak Your truths whenever situations attempt to silence me. In Jesus's name, amen.

KINGDOM KEY: Your voice matters; don't muzzle the message God placed in you.

seventy-nine

Soul Food

A folklore and myths course is a requirement for me to move on to the next semester, and a point of study is the Bible. While I don't refer to the Bible as fantasy literature, I won't be able to defend my faith. I don't understand the Bible, nor do I have much interest in it. Netflix is far more satisfying to me. —*the girl who finds the Bible boring*

Hey girl,

The world has been blinded to the truth of God altogether, but we believers often cannot swallow the truth because we are not aware of its depths. We ruin our appetites with too much of the wrong things.

The Bible is not out of touch or make-believe. Throughout the centuries, God has ensured that His Word remains indestructible so that it can lead us now as we search for wisdom and understanding. "For the word of God is alive and active. Sharper than any double-edged sword, . . . it judges the thoughts and attitudes of the heart" (Heb. 4:12 NIV). We are lying to ourselves if we listen to the Word being preached but don't apply it to our lives. If we love Christ, we will obey His teaching.

Is the lack of the Word of God in your life convicting you that your heart isn't yet devoted to Christ? Then ask the Holy Spirit to increase your desire for God and His Word! He will open your eyes and ignite a fire in you. When you delight in the Word of God, you will love differently, forgive differently, and witness differently. It will transform you from the inside out.

SCRIPTURE: "Open my eyes to see the miracle-wonders hidden in your word. My life on earth is so brief, so tutor me in the ways of your wisdom." (Ps. 119:18–19 TPT)

DIG DEEPER: Psalm 119:14–20; John 14:23; James 1:22

PRAYER: Father, I admit I don't want to read the Bible, but today I ask for forgiveness and for a thirst for Your Word. Soften my heart; give me the love I don't have. Help me to make a radical change in my habits. Bring me revelation so that I may live and breathe Your truth. You said one who takes heed of Your Word builds their house on a rock. Father, be my foundation. In Jesus's name, amen.

KINGDOM KEY: Scripture is soul food. Get your intake of "daily bread," so opinions and distractions can't spoil your appetite.

eighty

The Good Old Days

It's days like today when I wonder if God even knows what He's doing. Like, why does every aspect of my life have to be some big unnecessary struggle? I miss how things used to be.
—*the girl feeling wistful*

Hey girl,

The Israelites felt the same way. After they had been enslaved to the Egyptians for over four hundred years, God set them free from slavery, free to worship Him, and free to live again. With Moses as their leader, they journeyed a long and hard way, but God was with them. However, God's people often forgot about His goodness while they were in the wilderness.

After only a month and a half of freedom, they groaned to the point of wishing they had died in captivity. God was pulling them into the promised land, yet they kept looking back, longing for Egypt.

We often recall our past through rose-colored lenses too. We moan and groan in our misery, but when God delivers us, we miss the comfort and familiarity our pain blanketed us with. When living in a disorienting present, we forget what God has freed us from, making it harder to look forward to what He's leading us to.

But God has the power to split open seas, lead out of the wilderness, and move mountains for His children. The grass will always be greener right where we allow God to act on our behalf. Our faith grows when we trust God with our unknown futures.

SCRIPTURE: "Don't ask, 'Why were things better in the old days than they are now?' It isn't wisdom that leads you to ask this!" (Eccles. 7:10 GW)

DIG DEEPER: Isaiah 42:9; Philippians 3:13–14

PRAYER: Father, may I walk in wisdom and not disillusionment. You took me out of that prison, freeing me in ways I could never imagine, and yet here I am, wanting to go back. Give me a spiritual perspective. Even when I don't see what You're doing now, give me the faith to know that it is always for my good. In Jesus's name, amen.

KINGDOM KEY: God was on the move back then, and God is on the move now.

eighty-one

Be Your Own Sunshine

I'm in a rut and I'm having a rough time getting out of it. I know it's unrealistic for me to feel like it's me against the world, but sometimes I feel like it is when the people I typically turn to cannot be there. —*the girl raining on her own parade*

Hey girl,

It's not always clear skies and sunny days. We all have our off days, and sometimes the worst ones seem to last the longest. Sometimes the dark clouds stay put, looming over our heads, sprinkling rain at any attempt to move forward.

As humans, we're prone to feel bad for ourselves. Whether the pain comes from an outside source or from within, self-pity sure has a way of making us comfortable. And while it can be comfortable, it is also dangerous, becoming a hindrance to what God wants to do in our lives.

Sometimes you need to hear encouragement from a friend, but sometimes you have to encourage yourself! Yes, shine bright for others, lead by example, love and live loud. But God has also called you to do and be those things for yourself.

When you place your hope, confidence, and sunshine in someone else and they leave, what are you to do? Are you going to stay empty because your main source of light doesn't shine for you anymore? Or are you going to get back up and be your own sunshine for the world to see?

SCRIPTURE: "David was greatly distressed, for the people spoke of stoning him, because all the people were bitter in soul, each for his sons and daughters. But David strengthened himself in the Lord his God." (1 Sam. 30:6 ESV)

DIG DEEPER: Nehemiah 8:10; Psalm 46:1–3; Isaiah 60:1; Ephesians 6:10

PRAYER: Heavenly Father, I know life won't always be like this—give me the strength to encourage myself. Teach me to fill myself up with Your Word so that You may light up my world with Your presence. May Your Spirit illuminate my entire being so that people are drawn to You. In Jesus's name, amen.

KINGDOM KEY: You may not have clear skies, but God will part the clouds to show you His Son.

eighty-two

The One

I want a guy to take me out and treat me nice. I want a guy who'll pick up my favorite flowers and food just because. I want a guy who sees me for me and loves me for it. I don't feel as special being single; I feel incomplete. —*the girl tired of being a third wheel*

Hey girl,

You are seen and you are loved, just as you are. And you are not alone; God's Spirit happily accompanies you. You are deserving of a man who loves you like Christ loves the church, so do not settle out of impatience or pressure. Do not compromise your standards or beliefs. Do not awaken love before its time.

Singleness is a season in which to flourish. It is an opportunity to discover who you are called to be. It is a time to draw near to God and accomplish the special missions He puts on your heart. Don't wait for someone to come along to treat you well—do it yourself! Take yourself out on a date; fall in love with God and fall in love with *you*. "You don't have to be lonely when you learn how to enjoy your own company."[6] And you don't have to feel like you're lacking when Christ becomes your first true love.

I know singleness may feel like a journey that never ends, but I can attest that learning who you are and embracing the process fully is worth experiencing. Being in a relationship does not define you—being God's child does. There is no other half; you are made whole in Him.

SCRIPTURE: "Oh, let me warn you, sisters in Jerusalem, by the gazelles, yes, by all the wild deer: Don't excite love, don't stir it up, until the time is ripe—and you're ready." (Song of Sol. 2:7 MSG)

DIG DEEPER: Proverbs 21:5; Song of Solomon 8:4; Colossians 1:10

PRAYER: Father, the wait is difficult. But first I want to get to the place where I'm satisfied with You. Teach me how to love You better and in turn love myself. Show me how I can enjoy and honor this process as I pursue You on my own. Thank you for the comforting reminder of how Christ completes me. In Jesus's name, amen.

KINGDOM KEY: Being in a relationship does not define you—being God's child does. There is no other half; you are made whole in Him.

6. Saint-Elien, *Claim Your Crown*, 177.

eighty-three

Just a Little Bit Longer

It's really hard to take in the thought that a thousand years to us is basically a day to God. It's hard when I consider how long I've been waiting and praying—for months and years. How is that barely a second to Him?! This struggle has lasted forever, and it's way too long for me. —*the girl feeling antsy*

Hey girl,

God's clock is different from ours, but He is not slow in keeping His promises! When He doesn't take us out of situations right away, it is because He is providing us an opportunity to experience joy on a new level.

While you wait on your miracle, don't stop working. When you have trouble, don't forget you are being tested so that your faith may grow. We mustn't be tired of doing what is pleasing unto the Lord. We mustn't give up because at the right time— His time—we will reap a great harvest of blessing.

As you are counting on God for something, He is working on developing your endurance in full so that you will be perfect and complete, needing nothing.

SCRIPTURE: "So let's not get tired of doing what is good. At just the right time we will reap a harvest of blessing if we don't give up." (Gal. 6:9)

DIG DEEPER: James 1:2–4

PRAYER: God, Your timing is always right, especially when mine is not. Give me endurance to withstand the waiting room. When I can't feel You working, may I stand on the knowledge of who I know You to be: honest, true, and the God of miracles. In Jesus's name, amen.

KINGDOM KEY: God will give you endurance to withstand the waiting room.

eighty-four

Reality Check

I have the power to ruin a good moment with one disillusioned, sarcastic remark. It's what I'm known for; I'm a cynic. Better yet, I'm a realist with a dash of pessimism. I believe in God and Jesus too. But I also believe in right here and right now. And right here, right now, there are very real problems with very real solutions that don't quite involve my faith. I'm not always going to look at the sunny side of every situation. Sometimes there simply isn't one. —*the girl who's the comedian you didn't hire*

Hey girl,

You are right. There is more than what meets the eye. However, negativity doesn't bring about the full picture. God sees all things and can bring you revelation. When you accept Christ and begin to live with eternity in mind, your perspective changes. Over time you see how faith is always a part of the picture when you look through spiritual lenses.

Following Christ isn't fluff. Heaven isn't la-la land where angels lie around strumming harps and shooting arrows. God doesn't expect us to live our lives with our heads in the clouds now, either.

He does, however, want our eyes fixed on Him as we venture through the adversities and even the menial moments of our every day. He is true. He is honorable and right and pure and lovely and admirable. He is excellent and worthy of praise.

So the next time you are tempted to focus on the negatives, remember, there is sin in our cynicism. When people look to you, may they see the promise of God, not pessimism.

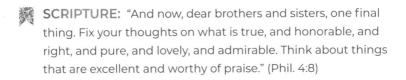 **SCRIPTURE:** "And now, dear brothers and sisters, one final thing. Fix your thoughts on what is true, and honorable, and right, and pure, and lovely, and admirable. Think about things that are excellent and worthy of praise." (Phil. 4:8)

 **DIG DEEPER:** Psalm 118:24; Proverbs 17:22; Philippians 4:4–9

PRAYER: God, I get it. Cynicism brings about negative images, and staying in dark rooms forever brings about distorted views. I don't want to be a killjoy; I'd rather bring joy. Forgive me, Lord. I've gotten faith all wrong. Help me to see life from the perspective of heaven. Thank you for giving me the chance to look at life again. In Jesus's name, amen.

KINGDOM KEY: Fight cynicism by counting on who God is.

eighty-five

Level Up

Now that I'm saved, I'm supposed to know what my gifts are and use them. I'm supposed to hear God more. I shouldn't be struggling with the same things. Life shouldn't be more difficult.
—*the girl who feels ripped off*

Hey girl,

You were not ripped off; God is ripening your fruit. At first you were a baby in the faith, and so you were fed milk and nursed on the elementary truths of God's Word. But as you mature spiritually, you are being fed real food, solids, as you apply His Word every day. But these things can be harder to swallow. Spiritual growth does not come easily. Sometimes you will choke or have hiccups. You will feel frustrated with your lack of progress, but one way to know you're heading in the right direction is if you bear the fruit of the Spirit. God is the gardener, Jesus is the vine, and the Holy Spirit produces the fruit. After you accepted Jesus and were born again, God gifted you with the Holy Spirit to help you in your journey.

The Spirit will take us from laying on our backs like a baby to sitting up to standing. And then we'll be walking and running, leaping and soaring. We will also stumble and fall. But knowing what we do, we won't go back to baby steps. We will look to our Father, who will pick us up again.

SCRIPTURE: "But solid food is for the mature—for those whose senses have been trained to distinguish between good and evil." (Heb. 5:14 CSB)

DIG DEEPER: John 15:5; Hebrews 5:13–14

PRAYER: Father, apart from You, I can't do anything! I can't grow on my own, but I can be intentional in spending time in Your presence to obtain the nourishment I need. I don't want to drift away from what I've already learned; I pray for more fruit so that I never return to elementary lessons. Life won't get easier, but it will get brighter with You as my light. The more I seek You, the more I find You. Thank you for the opportunity to know You better. In Jesus's name, amen.

KINGDOM KEY: Keep your roots planted in good soil and tilt your face toward the sky. We were called to sprout up into the fullness of Christ.

eighty-six

Heart Check

Have you ever said something that shocked everyone, including yourself? Ever wondered where that hostility came from? My mouth betrayed me, and I'm not quite sure why I said what I did. I just had an outburst out of nowhere, and I didn't know I had it in me. —*the girl who just exploded*

Hey girl,

We often don't notice the offenses we keep. Sometimes we don't realize that we're hurt. We allow the hurts to pile up until they influence our speech and then, later, our everyday lives.

But the mouth speaks what the heart is full of. Unforgiveness can breed hatred and can stop you from living freely. Envy, jealousy, fear, anger, hate—the list goes on. What they all have in common is the way in which they sap you of your strength and attention.

You'll be surprised at how sin has the power to shape what you do and say until you step back and evaluate your life. The best way to free up your space is by asking God to search you.

He doesn't look at you through a human perspective; He peers into your heart.

Ask yourself, what exactly is God seeing when He's looking on the inside? Is it resentment? Brokenness? Pride? Whatever it is, He wants to rid you of it all. Don't allow a dirty heart to disqualify you from moving forward with a renewed spirit and lasting life change.

SCRIPTURE: "Search me, God, and know my heart; test me and know my anxious thoughts. See if there is any offensive way in me, and lead me in the way everlasting." (Ps. 139:23–24 NIV)

DIG DEEPER: 1 Samuel 16:7; Luke 6:45

PRAYER: Father, forgive me for neglecting matters of my heart. Search me and expose the areas that need working on. Show me where I need to grow. Uproot the hurt and plant seeds of healing. Do the work in me. In Jesus's name, amen.

KINGDOM KEY: Don't allow a dirty heart to disqualify you from moving forward with a renewed spirit and lasting life change.

eighty-seven

Behind the Scenes

I've been working tirelessly on special projects, and I'm so excited to share the finished product. But that's the thing: I'm not finished. It's difficult getting on social media without having anything to show for it. While everyone is posting their new podcasts, videos, blogs, and creative TikToks, I'm left looking like I've been doing nothing, even though I'm actually doing so much behind the scenes. —*the girl with everything to prove*

Hey girl,

Here are three things to keep in mind:

1. God sees all you're doing.
2. Preparation is just as important as execution.
3. As you're working toward the finished product, God is also working on you.

The projects, the studying, the job—whatever you're putting your all into—may not be announcement-worthy now, but it's also something that likes, comments, and retweets can't ever measure up to.

To the outside world, you may not have much to show for what you're working on—your own mind may even trick you into believing it! But trust that the fruits of your labor will be realized. Not just for you, no. God's glory will always be revealed for all to see.

Take comfort in the fact that He sees the work you're putting in behind the scenes.

SCRIPTURE: "Therefore, my dear brothers and sisters, stand firm. Let nothing move you. Always give yourselves fully to the work of the Lord, because you know that your labor in the Lord is not in vain." (1 Cor. 15:58 NIV)

DIG DEEPER: Psalms 27:13; 128:2

PRAYER: Heavenly Father, You know my heart. I'm not looking to show off; I'm looking to show up. I want to show the world what I'm doing for Your glory; I want to prove that though it's not something I can post, it's a project deserving of praise. Lift me in my discouragement; may I look forward to Your reward alone. In Jesus's name, amen.

KINGDOM KEY: The fruits of your labor will be realized for the glory of God.

eighty-eight

No More Excuses

It's all fun until you're caught red-handed. But really, I'm not the bad guy here! I keep allowing myself to get caught up in their games, and I'm the only one who always suffers, always loses. They are the ones to blame. *—the girl without accountability*

Hey girl,

Sometimes, it's not them. Sometimes, the real problem is what you've done. It's time to stop making excuses and attempting to justify your cause. It's time to own up. Sin seems fun when we're in it, but not when we sit on the knowledge that God sees. He knows how we got in the mess and honors us when we humble ourselves and are accountable for our faults.

Putting on the coat of humility does not cover us from the consequences of previous wrongs; however, it relaxes God's hand. It is His nature to respond to the humility He so values with His redeeming love and power.

It's not too late to be redeemed. It's not too late to be transformed. It doesn't matter what you did or how you got there.

When you display your humility, like a good Father, God will douse you with His mercy and grace.

SCRIPTURE: "Humble yourselves, therefore, under God's mighty hand, that he may lift you up in due time." (1 Pet. 5:6 NIV)

DIG DEEPER: Luke 14:11; Philippians 2:3–4; Hebrews 4:13

PRAYER: Father, forgive me for not being accountable. Humility draws me near to You, but this entire time I allowed my pride to push me away. You're willing to lift me up, but I've allowed myself to get in the way. Show me how to make humility a habit as I seek You more and more every day. In Jesus's name, amen.

KINGDOM KEY: The coat of humility does not cover us from the consequences of previous wrongs, but it relaxes God's hand.

eighty-nine

Delayed Obedience

I don't want to do it. And now, my mind is playing tricks on me, as if the push I feel to act is all in my head. But if the idea—that I truly dislike, I must add—really is my own, I can move on and live my life; I wouldn't feel guilty about *not* accomplishing the task. But if it's God's idea, why would He have me do that? For what reason? —*the girl confused about the message*

Hey girl,

God is not a god of confusion. If you need clarity, ask. But I can say from experience that when we feel an urge to do something that's out of our comfort zone, that's often God giving the direction, not us.

Most recently He told me to do something I wasn't very familiar with—something I didn't want to do. He instructed me to "go live" on Instagram and share a message without any notes or preparation. He instructed me to depend on Him fully.

Now, if you know me, the request to show up unprepared is baffling. I am a planner to a T! But God will prepare us for the thing He tells us to do. We must first show up. Another thing

God is teaching me is that the message is already in me, and so, I am here to tell you it's in you too.

God may not be calling you to "go live," but He is calling you to go deeper with Him. He's calling you out of fear and into His arms. He is calling you to speak up, even if that means your heart is crying out to Him.

Don't allow anything to hold you back from what God said the first time. Don't look for a way out—commit to what He tells you when He shows you the signs that you ask for. There's too much at stake when we hesitate. Delayed obedience is still disobedience to Him.

 **SCRIPTURE:** "Whoever heeds discipline shows the way to life, but whoever ignores correction leads others astray." (Prov. 10:17)

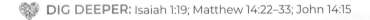 **DIG DEEPER:** Isaiah 1:19; Matthew 14:22–33; John 14:15

PRAYER: God, I don't want to doubt Your voice. May I no longer ignore Your call but instead commit to it. Yes, I did hear You the first time, but thank you for being willing to give me confirmations. I won't allow fear or pride to paralyze me anymore. I will do what You say the first time. In Jesus's name, amen.

KINGDOM KEY: Will you allow room for God's Spirit to move through your limitless "yes"?

ninety

Treasure Hunts

With the pressures of life, I feel like either I'm hunting for perfection or I'm the one being hunted. The world wants so many pieces of me, and I'm tired of giving myself away. I don't want to get to the place where I can't be rebuilt again, but I'm stuck.
—*the girl on a hunt*

Hey girl,

Humankind enjoys treasure hunts. Wouldn't you agree?

From childhood, we're taught to find the perfect pieces to put the cardboard puzzle together. As we mature, we attempt to do this with our hearts. We live in constant pursuit of the part that fits, knowing that there is more to life. That there is something missing.

And there is. We know there is more because God created us with the desire for eternity. Ecclesiastes 3:11 says, "He has made everything beautiful in its time. He has also set eternity in the human heart; yet no one can fathom what God has done from beginning to end" (NIV).

So you see, there isn't a problem with you. The void you have is intentional; it can be filled only with something bigger, and it's up to you to choose. Some select relationships, money, work, or themselves. But would you rather ram an obtuse piece into your heart, twisting and turning it, forcing it to fit?

Or do you want to fill your heart with what it was actually meant for?

Wanna strike gold? You will finish the treasure hunt only when you fill yourself with the Father.

SCRIPTURE: "For God so loved the world that he gave his one and only Son, that whoever believes in him shall not perish but have eternal life." (John 3:16 NIV)

DIG DEEPER: Exodus 34:6; Psalms 81:10; 103:5; 107:9

PRAYER: God, I've been searching when You've already found me. I've been running, and still You pursued me. Thank you for loving me so much that You sent Your one and only Son to die for my sins. I'm grateful for this second chance at life. Today and forever, I choose You. In Jesus's name, amen.

KINGDOM KEY: The tomb was empty so that we could be made full. In Christ we are complete!

ninety-one

Go to Bed

I'm a go-getter and a perfectionist with multiple hustles—that can sometimes be a horrible mix. I like things done correctly, and I'm always looking for ways to improve creatively and professionally, but I'm drained. I'm exhausted as I work on that project no one in my group showed up to do the night before. I'm constantly watching the clock at work, and I can't even enjoy being home. I force myself to work on the ideas I have brewing inside me, but by the time I hit the shower, all of my inspiration is gone. I stay up extremely late only to feel dissatisfied with what I've done. I wish I had the time to do what I wanted to do and keep up with all the other creators on social media.—*the girl who values work over sleep*

Hey girl,

I am a full advocate of "you gotta do what you gotta do," but it is the worst feeling ever to spread yourself thin. In doing the most, you hold yourself back.

Step away from it all and allow God to create your schedule. I know, I know. It sounds crazy. Many of us feel we can't afford the luxury of taking a break, but you don't need a spa for self-care. It's honestly the simple things, like putting work aside and taking a deep breath. It's releasing all your stressors into the hands of your loving Father.

We're so accustomed to doing that we never allow ourselves to just be. But God wants you to live. He wants you to walk by faith in order to fully experience His peace. God doesn't want you to play catch-up with the world; He wants you to wait on Him.

It's time to experience life right where you are. Be present with your family and friends and be honest with yourself. Give it all to God and then go to bed!

SCRIPTURE: "Lead me in your truth and teach me, for you are the God of my salvation; for you I wait all the day long." (Ps. 25:5 ESV)

DIG DEEPER: Psalm 127:2; Proverbs 16:3; Ecclesiastes 5:12; Micah 7:7

PRAYER: Heavenly Father, please take control of my life; I'm tired of taking the lead. I desire to do Your will and to just be. Fill my agenda with Your plans for me and give me solace as I wait on You. In Jesus's name, amen.

KINGDOM KEY: God doesn't want you to play catch-up with the world; He wants you to wait on Him.

ninety-two

Seasonal Friendship

Someone I never thought would leave my side . . . did. We had a great relationship, so her actions are really unexpected. We shared prayer requests, problems, and life experiences—she was like a sister. I reached out to ask her what's going on. She smiled and said everything was okay, but it's clear she's purposely distancing herself. I'm okay with letting the friendship die. I'm just confused as to why it had to happen at all. —*the girl who's stepping back*

Hey girl,

You won't always understand why some people act the way they do, and you don't need all the answers. Some dying relationships don't need a reason. Sometimes it's just the season.

When it's time to let go, allow life to take its course. Your friend may have personal issues she has to deal with, and she'll share on her own terms if she's willing. You did your part by extending love and checking in. Don't focus on what went wrong if you have no idea and she doesn't want to share. Put your efforts into forgiving her instead.

I'm sorry that it hurts and you're confused. But God will put lasting friends in your life—ones who won't leave you pondering where you stand. "God knows you need covenant friends for what He has called you to do."[7] He has set aside people who are meant to be your spiritual partners and who will do life with you.

And the best part is this: God is open and honest. He is a faithful friend forever.

SCRIPTURE: "So this is my command: Love each other deeply, as much as I have loved you. For the greatest love of all is a love that sacrifices all. And this great love is demonstrated when a person sacrifices his life for his friends." (John 15:12–15 TPT)

DIG DEEPER: 1 Samuel 18–20

PRAYER: Father, thank you for being the best friend I could ever have. Teach me how to open up to You and share my secrets. Help me run to You before approaching anyone else. I understand You will provide friendships that not only are pleasing to You but also will last. May I guard my heart but still love freely. In Jesus's name, amen.

KINGDOM KEY: Friendships come and go, but we have a forever friend in King Jesus.

7. Saint-Elien, *Claim Your Crown*, 102.

ninety-three

Open Doors

I missed it. I knew I should've jumped on the offer when I had the chance, and now it's gone. For so long, I felt as if doors kept shutting in my face. Now the one opportunity I was presented with is no longer an option for me. How'd I let that one slip through my fingers? —*the girl beating herself up*

Hey girl,

Closed doors are for your protection. So really, you didn't miss anything. Oftentimes we ignore God's warnings and force ourselves into situations He never called us to. We willingly walk into a world of confusion and struggle when we fail to discern which doors are from our heavenly Father. But just because something is a good thing doesn't mean He's the one who gave it.

When you are in the same room with God, He will always help you enter the right door. Nothing will pass you by because whatever He has for you is for you. He has positioned you where you are right now, but you're so focused on the next thing that you don't realize there are action items you have neglected to complete.

As God's children, we live by the Spirit's power; we are not powerless. We have access to the unimaginable with Him. But first you must make the most out of where you are. Grab the blessing—yes, the one you weren't aware of—and build. When you walk in His will, you will be pushed in the proper direction and pace.

SCRIPTURE: "So be careful how you live. Don't live like fools, but like those who are wise. Make the most of every opportunity in these evil days. Don't act thoughtlessly, but understand what the Lord wants you to do." (Eph. 5:15–17)

DIG DEEPER: Psalm 25:12; Proverbs 19:20; Isaiah 30:18–21; Jeremiah 33:3

PRAYER: Father, teach me to have grace for myself. I'm tired of my mind replaying the things I didn't do. I don't want to live with the fear of missing out. There's nothing I can miss if I'm focused on You. Give me discernment so that I am able to differentiate between good opportunities and God opportunities. I aim to take heed of Your warnings and stray from what the world says is good for me. In Jesus's name, amen.

KINGDOM KEY: When we walk in His will, we will be pushed in the proper direction and pace.

ninety-four

There's No Competition

I'm not comfortable sharing my achievements with my best friend. I noticed rather quickly that on the rare occasion I mustered up some excitement to share good news, she would attempt to smile and then quickly change the subject. But I've kept my accomplishments to myself for so long, I've come to realize that I no longer know how to celebrate myself. Instead, I look for ways to celebrate her.—*the girl rooting for everyone but herself*

Hey girl,

God created you to light up the world, and it's a radiant sight the way we all shine differently. If a friend can't understand you can both do that together, then that person isn't really for you.

People will look at you and see God's glory—and some may root against you because of it. Unfortunately, this can include those closest to you. Not everyone is willing to put aside competition and comparison, though sometimes it's not their fault. Sometimes jealousy and insecurity hold them captive.

The world advises you to keep your friends close and your enemies closer, but God says be watchful and love your enemies wholeheartedly, while remembering He called you out from where you were, to be who He has called you to be.

SCRIPTURE: "There are 'friends' who destroy each other, but a real friend sticks closer than a brother." (Prov. 18:24)

DIG DEEPER: 2 Kings 2; Job 42:10; Proverbs 27:9; Ecclesiastes 4:9–12; 1 Thessalonians 5:11

PRAYER: Father, thank you for bringing me out of darkness and into Your light. Expose the areas of my relationships that are unhealthy. Show me how to shine boldly in the midst of situations that aim to discreetly dim me. May I continue to uplift others as You uplift me. You have created me to shine, and I will do just that, no matter anyone's comfortability. In Jesus's name, amen.

KINGDOM KEY: God created you to light up the world.

ninety-five

Are You Done Yet?

It's not fair—my life never is. Nothing ever goes my way. Nothing ever works out for me. I have to struggle over every little thing. Everyone is living their best lives, and I'm just barely getting by. I'm sick and tired of it. Everything agitates me. And did you see this weather? I'm over it; I'm over them; I'm over you. —*the girl with a list of complaints*

Hey girl,

I know God looks down at us and has to repeatedly say, "Are you done yet?" He created you with beautifully complex feelings and enjoys your expressiveness. You can be angry and frustrated—it's healthy to let it out. But what He finds unhealthy and even sinful is your complaining.

You may think your grumbling is no big deal, but it's one of the most overlooked sins. It's easy to indulge in because complaining with others forges connections. But that's the opposite of what He purposed you to do. Picking your life apart and finding fault in everything do not lead you to His peace or the contentment found in Christ alone. And a sour and pessimistic view dampens your testimony.

In a world where people have issues with many things, God urges us not to join in. Instead, shine brightly before those around you so your commendable actions will illuminate the world. When you choose to sit out your own pity party, you publicly honor Christ. Turn your complaints into conversations about the good news of His love.

SCRIPTURE: "Do everything without grumbling and arguing, so that you may be blameless and pure, children of God who are faultless in a crooked and perverted generation, among whom you shine like stars in the world." (Phil. 2:14–15 CSB)

DIG DEEPER: Exodus 16:8; Numbers 11; James 5:9

PRAYER: Heavenly Father, forgive me for all the times I've done nothing but complain. I know I serve a good God who can and will help me guard my mouth. I want to find full contentment in You, Lord. I want to shine my light so that those around me will be drawn to You. How I respond to things is what differentiates me from the world, and I want to look like You. In Jesus's name, amen.

KINGDOM KEY: Picking your life apart and finding fault in everything do not lead you to God's peace.

ninety-six

Is Christ in Your Circle?

Most of my friends aren't Christian and that's fine, right? I mean, Jesus hung with sinners all the time, so why can't I? I have a few friend groups—church friends, work friends, school friends—it all works for me. I enjoy having different friends for different occasions. I have the best of both worlds. —*the girl who's a friend to everyone*

Hey girl,

Jesus is a friend of sinners, but there's more to it than that. His friends wanted what He had to offer. Jesus spent time with people who religious leaders and society looked down upon because He had love to give. His friends were open to His teaching, and they were willing to accept it. They were willing to believe.

The reputations of Jesus's friends were not a secret—they were dishonest tax collectors, prostitutes, and drunkards, but He welcomed them anyway. Their communities were drawn to their testimonies and inspired by their transformations and their faith and accessible power in Jesus.

You too can have that same impact. You have the power to influence anyone around you. You can't live your life devoted to Christ when living a double life. Be careful you don't adopt traits that drive you away from God.

Your friends should know who God is by how you live. God doesn't overlook sin—He is a holy God who forgives it.

SCRIPTURE: "But the Pharisees and their teachers of religious law complained bitterly to Jesus's disciples, 'Why do you eat and drink with such scum?' Jesus answered them, 'Healthy people don't need a doctor—sick people do. I have come to call not those who think they are righteous, but those who know they are sinners and need to repent.'" (Luke 5:30–32)

DIG DEEPER: Matthew 9:9–13; Luke 19:1–10; 1 Corinthians 15:33; 1 Timothy 1:15

PRAYER: Father, I am now mindful that if any of my circles do not include You, there's no reason I should be in it. Teach me to be bold with sharing Your love. I don't want to be influenced; I desire to leave Your mark. In Jesus's name, amen.

KINGDOM KEY: Your friends should know who Christ is by how you live.

ninety-seven

Temporary Home

Being the odd one out is isolating. When I open my mouth to say I'm a Christian, I realize just how hostile this world really is. I'm tired of being ostracized. I don't think I'll get desperate enough to do something just to fit in, but lately I've found myself wondering if this Christian thing is worth it. —*the girl who wants to feel like she belongs*

Hey girl,

When you don't feel like you belong, stand in the confidence of Whose you are. Being a Christian isn't just a title you wear; it's a way of life. You are a follower of Christ and were reborn in Him. You have a strong, eternal bloodline that links to your only hope, Christ Jesus. You are an heir to the kingdom of God with an inheritance that lasts forever. We serve a King who has the power to help us withstand persecution, and He always welcomes us into His company.

When God tells us to be in the world and not of it, He means that our identities must remain distinct in a land where there are many tantalizing, blurred lines. This life is temporary. We are only passing through as we prepare for a glorious eternity in heaven. Keep your eyes peeled for the city to come. We are chosen, cherished, and redeemed. Eternity is waiting; heaven is our home. We are misfits for the cause of Christ.

SCRIPTURE: "Just remember, when the unbelieving world hates you, they first hated me. If you were to give your allegiance to the world, they would love and welcome you as one of their own. But because you won't align yourself with the values of this world, they will hate you. I have chosen you and taken you out of the world to be mine." (John 15:18–19 TPT)

DIG DEEPER: Philippians 3:20; Hebrews 13:14; James 4:4–8

PRAYER: Heavenly Father, help me to live a life that's pleasing to You. When feelings of isolation come, help me to immerse myself in You, to journey with a community of believers, and through it all to always remember that this world is temporary. Because of the knowledge of who I am, I can live an abundant life as a nomad who will always fit in Your arms. It is an honor to call You Father; it is an honor to call You my home. In Jesus's name, amen.

KINGDOM KEY: When you don't feel like you belong, stand in the confidence of Whose you are. Heaven is your home.

ninety-eight

Purity, Not Perfection

You know the beatitude that talks about how the pure in heart will see God? How in the world is that going to happen for me?! I'm too far from perfect; I'm a hot mess from the inside out.
—*the girl who thinks purity is impossible*

Hey girl,

What if I told you that not only society but also the church gets the concept of purity wrong a lot of the time?

According to David, known as the man after God's own heart, purity is truthfully seeking the face of the Lord. James tells us a pure heart is an undivided heart; it is total allegiance to King Jesus. Through my own experiences, I've learned a pure heart is the willingness to change, the willingness to serve and obey. It is the willingness to ask God to search our hearts, cleanse them, and lead us in ways everlasting.

No one else may know your deepest, darkest secrets, thoughts, and feelings, but God sees you for who you really are, and He can handle the condition of your heart. Christ wasn't

crucified simply to correct bad habits; He came for total transformation from the inside out.

God gives us grace for the times we fall and allows us back
into His presence again and again. None of us are perfect, but
through Christ we have the power to overcome anything that
is not like our God. Purity, or a life of holiness, does not mean
perfection.

SCRIPTURE: "The purpose of my instruction is that all believers would be filled with love that comes from a pure heart, a
clear conscience, and genuine faith." (1 Tim. 1:5)

DIG DEEPER: 1 Samuel 16:7; Psalm 24:3–6; Matthew 5:8

PRAYER: Father, thank you for not holding me to impossible
standards. I'm far from perfect, so I'm grateful for Your grace
and the cleansing agent of salvation. I am honored to have
the opportunity to see You. Thank you for Your Holy Spirit who
is cultivating an open, undivided heart that chases You. May I
be obedient in all You have called me to do. In Jesus's name,
amen.

KINGDOM KEY: Let go of the pressure to be perfect; the Holy
Spirit alone has the power to purify our hearts.

ninety-nine

Last Days

I'm petrified about what's going on in the world. Every time I catch a news headline, I'm filled with anxiety. I've been avoiding the book of Revelation—as if the longer I do, the more time we have on earth. But I don't want to be here when life is unbearable for the body of Christ. —*the girl who's scared about the last days*

Hey girl,

Life isn't a movie, and the best part is that we know what happens in the end! The book of Revelation is one of celebration. Yes, Christians will face persecution like never before. There will be battles, but God has already won the war. Because of our salvation, we won't perish—we were promised eternal life in the presence of true royalty.

It's hard to imagine what life will be like after this one. After all, this world is all we know! The enemy wants you to be frightened, but Revelation gives us a glimpse of a paradise too good to even fathom.

Ask God to stir up excitement in your spirit. Pray that you love Him more than you love the world. As you await the return of Christ, stay vigilant and spread His redemptive love everywhere you can. We don't know when Christ will come but take comfort in the fact that He's returning for a rescue mission, one we desperately need!

SCRIPTURE: "There will be strange signs in the sun, moon, and stars. And here on earth the nations will be in turmoil. . . . People will be terrified at what they see coming upon the earth, for the powers in the heavens will be shaken. Then everyone will see the Son of Man coming on a cloud with power and great glory. So when all these things begin to happen, stand and look up, for your salvation is near!" (Luke 21:25–28)

DIG DEEPER: Ephesians 1:11; Colossians 1:20; Revelation 1:7

PRAYER: Father, I desire to love You more than anyone or anything. Thank you that I will not perish but will one day hear You say, "Well done." Teach me how to best exemplify Your love to others and to stand firm as I await Your return. In Jesus's name, amen.

KINGDOM KEY: We don't know when, but Christ is returning for a rescue mission!

one hundred

Your Heavenly Crown

I thought entering the pearly gates was the primary goal of the Christian. What's this I hear about receiving crowns in heaven? And if I can receive rewards in heaven, is it possible to lose them too?—*the girl who doesn't want to let God down*

Hey girl,

First, I'd like to remind you that we gain eternal life when we accept Christ into our lives. We can't work our way into heaven; we are saved by the grace of God!

Having reestablished that, let me say that being in the presence of our King is the ultimate reward! Yet God loves us so much that He will also reward us with crowns based on our service and the suffering we experience in our earthly lives.

What we do (or don't do) on this earth dictates our rewards (or crowns) in heaven. The New Testament teaches that steadfast followers of Christ will receive crowns when He returns. There's an imperishable crown, the crown of life, the crown of righteousness, the unfading crown of glory, and so much more!

As believers, we must build for eternal rewards right now. Sin and an unrepentant heart are what stand in our way. But you won't let Him down because He is lifting you up. Consider what ways you can honor God through your life. Obedience to our King is what pleases Him.

SCRIPTURE: "Don't you realize that in a race everyone runs, but only one person gets the prize? So run to win! All athletes are disciplined in their training. They do it to win a prize that will fade away, but we do it for an eternal prize." (1 Cor. 9:24–25)

DIG DEEPER: Ephesians 2:8–10

PRAYER: Heavenly Father, thank you for lifting me up. What an honor it is to have the future privilege of seeing Your face and being rewarded for what You have called me to do. Lord, help me to remain steadfast. May faithfulness be ingrained in me as I follow You into forever. In Jesus's name, amen.

KINGDOM KEY: As believers, we must build for eternal crowns while there is still breath in our bodies.

There is no
other half;
you are
made whole
in Him.

Conclusion

Forever He Will

And I am convinced that nothing can ever separate us from God's love. Neither death nor life, neither angels nor demons, neither our fears for today nor our worries about tomorrow—not even the powers of hell can separate us from God's love. No power in the sky above or in the earth below—indeed, nothing in all creation will ever be able to separate us from the love of God that is revealed in Christ Jesus our Lord.

Romans 8:38–39

Hey girl,

As you go out into this world, lift up your head and steady your crown. The King of all kings is seated high and lifted up on the throne of your life. His Son, Jesus, is at His right hand interceding for you. They are looking down from heaven, rooting for you, gazing at you in love.

Our King sees all and will speak to you.

His Word will bring you hope and strength, and when you feel alone, His Spirit will provide you sweet company.

He will carry you and dote on you.

He will be with you in the worst of times and in the best of times.

He will never leave you or forsake you.

He will guide you and give you grace.

He will redeem you and release you from your pain.

He will pour His protection over you.

He will fill the gap of anyone who has neglected you.

He will be with you in life, and He will be with you in death, and nothing will separate you from His presence.

He will love you right now until death do us part and for all eternity.

When troubles come, do not fear, because He is with you. Do not be dismayed; after all, you serve the Almighty. He will strengthen you and bring you aid; He will sustain you with His righteous right hand (Isa. 41:10). Indeed, He is mighty to save and will rejoice over His precious daughter with gladness. He will hush you with an overwhelming love; He will sing over you with delight (Zeph. 3:17).

He is the Master over all and is faithful and glorious and still living today. He is God Most High and is merciful and just and mighty in battle. He is the holy God who sees you, bringing you refuge and strength. He is the everlasting God who is your exceeding joy, your salvation, and your rock. He is the Lord who blesses you, keeps you, shines upon you. He is the God of kindness, goodness, and truth. He is the Lord, mighty in battle, your redeemer, your fortress, and your shield. He is the Lord who delivers you, brings you healing, and provides for all of your needs. He is an all-consuming fire, but He is also your comforter and your friend and, yes, He is your Father. He is the Prince of Peace. He is the abiding, all-sufficient God, and He cannot wait to spend eternity with you.

When you said yes by accepting Christ Jesus, He promised you forever.

As you go through this life, He will be true to you and expects the same honor. Christ will return for the church, His bride, one day soon to invite us into His palace of many rooms. May He find your heart in the same posture as it was the first time you said, "I do."

Appendix

IDENTITY

INTIMACY

PAIN

PERSEVERANCE

TARAH-LYNN SAINT-ELIEN is a fierce and favored fashionista, inspiring thousands of women through her *Dressed for Battle* podcast and her brand, Adorned in Armor. Crowned Miss Black New Jersey in 2018, the Teen Vogue It Girl turned fashion writer graduated summa cum laude from Rider University and earned her master's degree from Syracuse University. Tarah-Lynn's features include CBN, the *Haitian Times*, and others! For additional inspiration about living with confidence and worth, check out Tarah-Lynn's debut book, *Claim Your Crown*, and the YouVersion devotional, which has over one hundred thousand completions around the globe. You can find Tarah-Lynn sharing her style, biblical affirmations, and teaching via Instagram (@adornedinarmor), YouTube, and adornedinarmor.com.

Connect with Tarah-Lynn

ADORNED in ARMOR

Dressed for Battle

@adornedinarmor
adornedinarmor.com

Join Tarah-Lynn on the
Dressed for Battle Podcast!

This is a Christian podcast that will equip you with the weapons to fight your battles and dream BIG. Armor up, girl! You were made to WIN.

What would your life look like if you truly believed you are *royalty*?

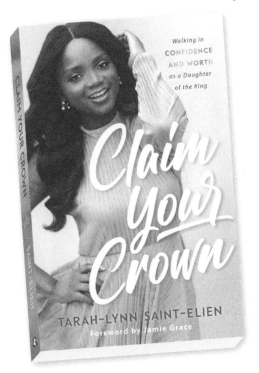

Claim Your Crown is your manual to unshakable confidence and an effective reign. Sharing her "kingdom keys," Tarah-Lynn offers soul-baring reflections, biblical encouragement, and unique insights on popular culture. Questioning our identity and worth ends here. It's time we rule.

Revell
a division of Baker Publishing Group
www.RevellBooks.com

Available wherever books and ebooks are sold.

Your voice is powerful;
let Tarah-Lynn show you how to believe in it!

The "Amplify Your Voice" workshop is designed to encourage you to believe in your God-given message so much that you're ready to share it with the whole world! Let's push ourselves to do what God has called us to, together.

www.adornedinarmor.com/courses